Dancing in My Grandfather's Garden

Unearthing the Soul of the Feminine
And the Gift of Deep Imagery

Phyllis Brooks Licis, MSW

Moon Bear Press

Dancing in My Grandfather's Garden

Unearthing the Soul of the Feminine
And the Gift of Deep Imagery
ISBN 13: 978-0-944164-18-1

Phyllis Brooks Licis, MSW

For information address
Moon Bear Press
PO Box 468
Velarde, NM 87582
USA

or email
orders@moonbearpress.com

Dancing in My Grandfather's Garden

Unearthing the Soul of the Feminine
And the Gift of Deep Imagery

Table of Contents

i   Preface

iii   Introduction

Part One   **Call of the Feminine**

1   Land of the Dead

13   The Descent

19   Communing with the Goddess

25   Lost Babies

29   My Womb Speaks

31   Sniffing Out My Path

Part Two   **Wild Tracks Within**

37   Entering the Ark

49   Loving My Majestic Being of Hate

55   A Place of Belonging

61   Wolf Mother

67   My Friend Turtle

Part Three   **Coming Home to My Soul**

77   Stripped of All My Regalia

85   The Spirit of Bear

87   Who Abandoned Whom?

91   Bee Juice

95   Reflection of the Feminine

101   Howling with Grey Wolf

105   Through the Eyes of Snake

109   Owning My Voice, Heart and Power with a Golden, Celtic Twist!

115   Leper Woman

127   Heart's Treasures

129   Afterward

133   Acknowledgements

137   About the Author

Preface

The heart has a nature that reason knows not of, to paraphrase the Great Bard. In our modern times we have lost our natural connection with our rootedness in Nature, in our wholeness and balance, and instead become tethered to what is currently mistaken for human. This would not be so bad if we at least remembered the return path. But we do not. Even so, the path back to our wholeness calls us, for as we become more and more distant from it the pain of having left it grows and grows. Our modern human tendency is to try to turn that pain off rather than to hear it and heed its call.

This book was written by a gentle and sensitive soul who heard and listened and dared. Her daring was not just for herself, for her own return to Center, but is a light that shows the way to what is possible. For the call of the Feminine, not just in women, but in men as well, is a deep invitation to return to balance, return to a life, aligned with the living nature in all of existence, including ourselves.

We have sacrificed that life to follow a map that does not fit. It does not fit not because it is wrong but because it is incomplete. It does not serve our wholeness, it does not provide a measure of who a human being is in ones entire depth, it is much too narrow to encompass the fullness of life. But we continue to pass on that map to our children thinking that they do not arrive with their own knowing but instead must be filled with ours.

The present book is a story, delicately told, of one woman's return, of her daring to listen with a sensitive ear, to that call that has echoed throughout our strange wanderings, and to her opening to the experience that is the only path back to Wholeness. One candle can fill an entire room with light. Phyllis Brooks Licis has done that with this lovely book. May this beautiful candle light your way as well.

Eligio Stephen Gallegos, PhD

Introduction

*The voice of the deep feminine calls to all men and women
to honor it and to usher it into the brilliant light of day.
There it can blossom, offering healing to the Earth and
all living things.   P. Brooks*

Some of us may have to go far in order to come
home. In a world that seduces us to the external by valuing
multi-tasking, busy schedules and measurable productivity,

how do we find our way back to our own inner path and true self?

For women in a culture that emphasizes *equality* for men and women, rather than *equal* but *very different*, that journey may require a deep search to find the inner feminine. Women growing up in this culture, with its focus on male-oriented thought processes and accomplishments, are bombarded daily with logic, clarity, order, fact and definition. We have adapted by taking on these modes of functioning as our own. We discipline our innate fluid depths and abandon our feminine instincts. They appear irrelevant in this rational world of facts and graphs.

Having turned our backs on our natural energy patterns, we have left dormant our inherent ability to sense the elemental energies of the world around us. Living in union with nature and the universe has become unfamiliar to us. Today, women's menses cycles rarely align with the cycles of the moon and with those of other women. The sacred dimensions of being a woman are no longer understood, no longer part of our lives. The authentic power of the feminine as protector, nurturer, mediator, visionary and vessel for new life has nearly vanished from our awareness.

Since there are no representations in our culture to reflect the full mystery and power of the feminine, it is difficult for us to live grounded in the authority of our own lives. We forget our deepest selves. We forget that there is a difference between knowing something intellectually and knowing intuitively.

"Successful daughters" of our culture, those who are

academically and professionally accomplished, are most at risk of following an externally driven path. If we bow to the expectations of our society, we will not truly flourish, we will not be authentically creative and our souls will not be at peace.

Alienated from my own feminine grounding, I found myself living, breathing and taking direction from my masculine side. The mysteries and deeper dimensions of the feminine were out of my reach, unknown and alien.

My life had always moved along as I thought it was meant to proceed. Raised in a hard-working family with strong moral fiber, where independence, the honor of one's word and service to others were key values, I internalized these standards.

Thinking that control and planning were essential factors for a happy and successful life, I worked diligently to keep my life predictable and controlled. My intellect served me well in this regard. Academic interests came easily to me. I loved solving problems and seeing the results. Knowing what it took to be successful, I set goals and took the necessary steps to achieve them. If something unpleasant happened, I didn't dwell upon it. I put it aside and continued with my pursuits.

A college education was not historically part of my family's vision for women, and so I washed dishes to augment my scholarships. Later, while doing post-graduate work at Boston University, I proudly aligned myself with the Women's Movement.

My understanding of being female was an intellectual one, which I came to see was a limited perspective. But life seemed right and comfortable. Living from my logical, rational side, the world of facts and proof, I felt competent, strong and accomplished.

Then one remarkable day I heard an undeniable cry from the feminine deep within. That cry stopped me in my tracks and turned my life upside down. I found myself in territory where my logical mind was not sufficient and I had to question everything I thought I knew.

I became aware of a desperate need to know the feminine as a living presence in my life, a transformative process exquisitely designed to guide me from my rational masculine view to a more authentic way of being. Only later did I comprehend that I had been invited on an inner quest to encounter the archetypal feminine and the soul dimensions of being a woman. That invitation would forever change my life!

When I was confronted with a series of pregnancies and losses, I attempted to cope by following my familiar, rational mode of behavior. In our achievement-oriented society, where results and worth are measured by products and outcomes, pregnancies that don't result in a living child are often ignored.

I pushed my feelings aside and moved on with "real life," that external world of plans and activity. I didn't listen to the feminine voice from within that told me to grieve. The loss, the pain, pushed down and silenced, nearly severed the frayed threads that connected me to the inner feminine.

Reconnecting with my inner feminine required me to relinquish my familiar goal-directed behavior and descend deep within to the unknown. The struggle between my masculine and feminine aspects led me to give birth to my true feelings, to my own voice and to myself as a woman and a mother.

My inward descent radically altered my perspective. I was awakened from a strictly intellectual knowing to an intuitive awareness. More diffuse, less measurable, but nevertheless strong and true, there is great power in the archetypal feminine and the life-giving soul dimensions of being a woman.

The healing of my inner feminine was circular, like the feminine process itself. Issues and feelings gently circled around, shifting, foreshadowing, rocking me, nudging me from the shadow to the light, as my feminine came into fullness.

This story is an account of my inner journey and a map to assist you in your own journeying. Together we'll travel to Ireland where, using a miraculous process called Deep Imagery, I was able to heal my losses and re-balance my inner feminine. I will share how memories of nature held within my body captured my attention and guided me back to life with the help of archetypal animal guides.

Collecting, embracing and releasing old feelings and emotions breathed new life into me and wove the feminine aspect permanently into the fabric of my being. It is vitally important for all of us, men and women alike, to value the feminine. It's this intuitive knowing, this quality of unconditional love, that is the only hope of saving the Earth and all of life.

We will find authentic meaning in our lives only through our own inner wisdom. It's time to reconnect with the instinctual feminine and re-discover an awareness that is very different from the intellectual.

Part One

Call of the Feminine

"On the wings of archetypal things, the sacred sleeps in you."
-Ariana Licis,
taken from her poem, "The Heart of All"

Land of the Dead

*A*s I walk forward in the dream, my grandfather comes to meet me. The light is low and he looks slightly different than usual, but I know it's him. His hair is longer and appears stringy. The area where he is standing is dark and unfamiliar to me, so it's difficult to see clearly.

I have always been drawn to my grandfather. I remember him in his denim overalls, work boots, and well-worn hat, limping slightly as he walked. He was a farmer and raised pigs.

As a child I wandered in his huge gardens, where vegetables and flowers were often taller than me. My favorite flowers, and his too, were the gladioli that triumphantly blew their message of beauty to the world. To walk with him was a magical gift, and his love for the Earth made it even more endearing.

I played at his piggery, climbing the fences, running among the high grasses, and skipping after the pigs. The smell of the rich fertile soil and the joy of my connection with nature saturated my heart and soul.

My grandfather was always laughing and joking and his eyes twinkled with delight. He spoke and moved with an earthy presence, always connecting fully with life. Sometimes he seemed larger than life itself. But tonight he is not smiling or laughing.

My grandfather wants my attention, and he has it.

Walking toward him, I see that his face is pale grey. He's gaunt and very thin, totally unlike his usual round, solid build. Each strand of his shoulder length hair seems tangled and thick. I stop, but he beckons me closer. As I hesitantly move forward, I feel a chill and hear the whisper:
"Land of . . ."

Uneasiness creeps up my back. I do not want to move, but something pulls me. I continue to inch closer. My grandfather lurches and falls forward, nearly landing on me. His hair, with the texture of cold, wet seaweed, slides across my face.

Suddenly, with a start of horror I realize I am in the "Land of the Dead."

When I woke from this dream about my grandfather, who had been dead for many years, I was badly shaken. The images haunted me for days. Finally, compelled by recurrences of this dream, I visited his piggery. The land had been sold years ago, and I hadn't seen the property since childhood.

A small house had been built on the land close to the road. As my eyes searched beyond the house, I saw the fields and fences near the adjacent woods. Farther back hunkered my grandfather's old shed, as if it were a permanent part of the Earth. I was mesmerized. I could practically hear my grandfather's voice, see the giant sunflowers and feel the rays of the sun. I watched butterflies flutter to and fro.

The whole scene was alive for me in a way it hadn't been for years, transporting my heart and soul back in time. My love for my grandfather, my connection to him and to the Earth washed over me in a warm wave.

So it was that by day, my heart and mind were filled with love and memories of my grandfather's life, and by night, my fear mounted as I dreaded a return walk through the Land of the Dead! Why was this happening and what did it mean? I had to find out.

This story actually began several years earlier, when I first met my husband, Guntis Licis. We immediately experienced an intense attraction for each other, as if we had been brought together by a cosmic magnet. Although neither of us had been searching for a serious relationship, it was clear that our paths had crossed for a reason, and that we were meant to be together. Guntis was divorced with a delightful, blond-haired, four-year-old son, Eriks. Eriks and I quickly became fast friends, enjoying each other's sense of humor and sharing a similar sensitivity for people and life.

Guntis and I dated, grew closer and moved in together. The bond between us felt timeless, as if we had always been together. In discussing our future, I was taken aback when Guntis adamantly stated that he did not want any more children. He loved his son and felt that dividing his time and energy would be unfair to Eriks. Never having particularly wanted children, I was shocked by how heavily his words landed upon my heart. One evening, I suddenly had an image of Guntis holding a baby girl – our daughter. I was surprised by this fleeting picture in my mind, but quickly dismissed it.

Loving and caring for Eriks slowly made me realize a formerly unacknowledged desire to conceive and bear a child and I anguished over Guntis' declaration. Gatherings where babies and young children were present became painful for me. Seeing pregnant women twisted my heart. Guntis and I discussed the issue, but he remained firm.

Attempting to deal "rationally" with the situation, using my logical, masculine tools, I began to believe that perhaps I wasn't meant to give birth to any children. Slowly and painfully, out of my love for Guntis and Eriks and my wish for us to be a family, I surrendered my dream. With a pre-nuptial agreement that we wouldn't conceive children,

Guntis and I made our wedding plans.

During supper, the night before our wedding, I playfully said, "Okay, anybody whose name is going to be Licis tomorrow, raise your hand!" With my hand in the air, I looked over at Eriks, expecting to see a smile and a raised hand. Instead, I saw that his face had dropped with disappointment. After a long silence, Eriks said, "I thought our names were going to be Brooks!!" I was touched beyond words, grateful that this beloved child wanted my name.

My love for Eriks and his adventurous spirit, guided me along the path of experiencing motherhood. We made cookies, played baseball, went camping and skiing. We decorated his room, shopped for school clothes, sang, laughed, talked and hugged. I became the mother of a Cub Scout, a student, an athlete. My heart was a mother indeed!

Four months after Guntis and I married, despite using a diaphragm, I became pregnant. With my logical mind intent upon honoring our marital agreement, I was naturally upset. And yet, deep in my body, in some part of me I'd never known, a spark of excitement flickered, hidden from my brain.

This was a moment when I might have looked within and wondered what was happening. Having taken all precautions against it, why was I pregnant? I didn't take the moment.

Guntis and I sought the assistance of a well-known Gestalt therapist to discuss the pregnancy, from "a here and now perspective." With her help, we decided that it "made sense" for me to have an abortion. If that hidden inner woman cried out in protest, I did not hear her.

Entering the clinic, my mind was taken back ten years to when I hadn't been married and had entered a similar clinic for the same procedure. I never expected to have another abortion, and certainly not when I was married.

This time, entering the clinic was easier emotionally, as my brain was clearly in charge of the day. "You agreed not to have children. Don't rehash it," I ordered myself sternly. When the doctor listened to my heart and discovered a murmur, he announced, "This abortion can not be done." He insisted on a series of antibiotics before the procedure. In a state of numb confusion, I slid off the table, got dressed, and went home.

Here was one more chance for me to look within and wonder, "What is happening? What is my heart murmuring?" But I didn't take it. Instead, I quickly obtained the antibiotics and had the abortion. Within a few days, life moved on. There were family and school events, preparing the boat for the spring launch, and the renovation of our home. I kept busy with "important" decisions and activities.

Three months later the Universe spoke to me once more: I was pregnant again! Too embarrassed to seek counseling a second time, and still believing that it was unfair to have a child if it was not desired by both parents, Guntis and I again decided to terminate the pregnancy.

Why a second pregnancy when I was trying so hard to prevent it? Was this just irresponsibility or was something else happening? I did not let myself hear the questions. The external world, my rational training and my masculine-oriented thought patterns still outweighed my inner world and I was herded along a preset path by the expectations of myself and others.

This time I felt very uneasy waiting at the clinic. Time seemed altered, as if I were moving slower than the rest of the world. My heart pounded as my eyes scanned the waiting area. I wondered about the other women sitting there. I studied their faces, watching every movement. I wondered about their stories.

When my name was called the uneasiness grew within me and I felt separated from my own body. Not understanding what I was feeling, I searched my rational mind for some explanation, but found none. The moment the procedure was finished, however, my feelings spewed out uncontrollably.

"Guntis, I am **never** doing this again!"

Life continued and these painful experiences and feelings withdrew to the recesses of my mind and heart. Externally focused, I busily placed my attention on finishing our home renovations. Baseball season started, and I was excited to be Little League Mother for Eriks's team.

It was one year after this second abortion that my Grandfather visited me from the Land of the Dead. During the year, I'd had a chorus of rumblings from within— sadness, fear, anger, confusion. Still vague feelings with no place to hang, they remained unidentifiable. Although I didn't understand this dream, its impact upon me made it clear that something beyond my normal, daily experience was demanding my attention.

I asked a colleague to recommend a therapist that he would see if he really wanted to make some changes in his life. On his recommendation, I sought the help of Dr. James Eckles, a wonderfully direct, out-spoken man who had studied at the Jungian Institute in Zurich.

From the very first visit, Dr. Eckles's drill-instructor demeanor and stern glance over the rim of his glasses, seemed to penetrate my soul. I was afraid to see him, but more afraid not to! Over the course of a year, Dr. Eckles walked with me through The Land of the Dead and other terrifying nightmares and confusing dreams.

It was a grueling inner search for an identity I'd never known. At times, I felt like a bareback rider, clutching for dear life the mane of a wildly galloping horse, knowing that all I could do was hold on for the ride.

My grandfather, who had been deeply rooted to nature, became an inner guide for me during this process.Beckoning me toward a more natural way of being, he accompanied me on an amazing journey through the archetypal. I began to recognize an illusive, feminine part of myself that I had never even suspected.

Wrestling the masculine, driven agenda that I had automatically absorbed as a child of our culture, I fought to retrieve my truth. I battled to uncover my feelings, confront my fear of the labor process and question my capacity to be a mother and my ability to birth a human baby. I struggled to re-create my relationship to myself as a woman. I descended into chaos.

Holding my process with respect and integrity, Dr. Eckles helped me save my life and my sanity as I attempted to untangle my inner world from my outer life and somehow find a way to honor them both. Eventually, I came to realize my truth. I had a profound need to create life within myself.

Owning and acknowledging my desire to myself was life altering, and I clearly felt the transformation. Having reconnected with my soul's need, I had a purpose and felt it intensely. Now my task was to gather up the courage to tell Guntis about my revelation.

The Universe demanded I acknowledge the deep feminine and speak my truth, and so I did. I could no longer hide it, either from myself or from Guntis. From the depths within me, with strength and clarity, I told him, "I want to be pregnant. I want and need to have a baby. I would love to have a child with you, Guntis, but if you don't want to, I will have a child elsewhere and with someone else. It is that important to me. It is that crucial to my soul!"

Having firmly spoken my truth from my inner feminine, it was no easy matter to negotiate. We separated and our hearts ached. We got back together. Guntis finally heard and recognized my need to have a baby, and he reluctantly agreed.

With the support of the Universe and Dr. Eckles, I had found and honored the feminine part of my being. From an authority deep within myself, I knew what I needed to do. I was filled with love for Guntis for having taken this leap of faith in our relationship. And I was grateful to my grandfather for having brought me back to life from the Land of the Dead.

"Gramps" feeding baby pigs

The Descent

*A*fter having two unplanned pregnancies while using birth control, I anticipated becoming pregnant quite easily. However, the Universe did not intend to let me off so lightly! As if my initial pursuit of my inner feminine was not difficult enough, I was challenged further. The Universe demanded that I embrace the feminine as part of my every-day life.

Thinking about my quest, I am reminded of one of the oldest known stories about transformation and embracing the feminine. Written on stone tablets in the third millennium B.C, this ancient Sumerian story of the Goddess Inanna-Ishtar, the Queen of Heaven and Earth, tells us that Inanna had an identity, a place and title on the Earth. Her life was full and joyful. But when she heard a call from Ereshkigal, the Queen of the Underworld, Inanna descended into the darkness to meet her shadow sister.

At each gate of the underworld, before Inanna was allowed to proceed, she was required to relinquish to the gatekeeper one of her silken veils, her magnificent jewels, her richly embroidered garments, her royal velvet robe. At the final gate, she fearfully handed over the golden breastplate protecting her heart. She was stripped of everything that represented her power in the upper world, everything that symbolized her safe, familiar identity and defenses. Humbled and vulnerable, she entered into the dark unknown, drawn to her shadow sister and the powerful process of opening to her own inner growth.

Like Inanna, I, too, descended. For two excruciating years, I tried to conceive but could not. Slowly stripped of all my identity and supports, humbled and vulnerable, I ventured down into the underworld—down into myself— to encounter the woman in the dark. No personal or professional accomplishments I had attained were relevant in this process, as I proceeded down through each gate toward my goal of pregnancy.

Relinquishing my familiar sense of being in control, I surrendered to a process in which I felt I had no control. I didn't know why I was incapable of accomplishing something every other woman seemed able to do without effort.

Lovemaking became hinged on temperature-taking, strategies, planning, and timing, which certainly hindered the romance, spontaneity, and mystery. I kept meticulous charts and records of my cycles and temperatures. My longing to be pregnant manifested physically, as each month I felt pregnant—believed I was pregnant! My breasts grew fuller, my nipples tender.

And then—the blood!

With every cell in my body, I experienced my monthly bleeding as a death, and mourned privately in the bathroom. In desperation, I wanted to reach down into the toilet and stuff the blood clots back into my body. I felt that intensely female grief which accompanies the fear of never being able to conceive. It was the early 1980's. People rarely spoke about infertility, and very few doctors specialized in this problem. Feeling alone and frustrated, I asked myself: What am I doing wrong? Why can't I get pregnant? Why had the Universe put me through such trials, only to mock me now?

I remembered going to parties years earlier and not having anything to contribute to the women's talk of babies and diapers. "How boring they are!" I thought, looking at the women as if from a great distance. Men's conversations about work, politics and achievements were much more interesting to me.

Now, all that seemed as distant as another life. Painfully, I watched my self-identity begin to shift. Dropping another silken veil, experiencing a whole new hunger inside of myself, I humbly found myself wanting to *be* one of these women. I even envied them!

Renouncing any last thread of belief in my will being able to accomplish pregnancy, fearing that I might never be able to conceive again, I passed through another gate and sought the help of a fertility specialist. Glancing at my beautifully designed temperature and monthly cycle charts, the doctor threw them on the floor, and said, "I don't understand what these charts mean!"

I was startled by his abruptness. In the past, out of desire for affirmation, my ego would have been insulted by his response. That day, however, I removed my richly embroidered garments of pride and protective anger and continued down through yet another gate. I listened and appreciated his straight forward style and un-flinching determination to help me conceive.

The first test to be done was a sperm count. It took all the will and courage I could muster to go to Guntis with this request. Having reluctantly agreed to have a baby, he had not included this test in his expectations. He quite reasonably felt it was an invasion, but loving me, knowing how desperately I wanted this, he acquiesced.

The tests indicated that sperm count wasn't the problem, so we moved on to test two. This one required me to watch the calendar and the clock. When the time of ovulation neared, Guntis and I had to make love within an hour of my appointment with the doctor!

During my examination, the doctor discovered no "viable" sperm. I knew what this meant, but asked the doctor about it anyway. "It means no pregnancy this month, and further tests to determine what is killing off the sperm."

The words "killing off the sperm" echoed in my ears and heart, as if in a canyon, reverberating loudly off stone, then dropping heavily to the bottom of my stomach. Staring at the cold walls of the doctor's office, I heard little else of what was said during the appointment, but wondered why my body was working against me.

The third test required was a biopsy of my uterus, an office procedure which was described as being "mildly uncomfortable." Expecting only mild cramping and perhaps a little staining, I was stunned by severe pain, intense bleeding, and a sick weakness that lasted for several days. But the weeks progressed and the pain diminished.

The next test was to be performed during my menses. I waited for that undeniable flag of death, but when the appointment day arrived, my menstrual period had not. I called the doctor to reschedule the appointment. Pausing a moment, he suggested that I have a pregnancy test before going any further.

"A pregnancy test? There were no viable sperm! How could I possibly be pregnant?" He re-stated his recommendation. Not understanding, but wanting to move forward, I proceeded to the lab for what seemed like a waste of time. That afternoon the doctor called.

I was pregnant!

Communing with the Goddess

*D*uring my pregnancy, I was convinced that I was beautiful! Watching my body change was like a miracle unfolding. What was happening to me was totally out of my control, yet somehow felt absolutely right. I was participating in a process, and at the same time the process was happening to me, within me, in spite of me! It was as if I were communing with the Goddess, connected to an archetypal energy, a strong inner feminine knowing that goes beyond time and space.

I knew that our baby was a girl, both from the dream work I did with Dr. Eckles and the vision I had early in my relationship with Guntis. So I wasn't surprised when the doctor confirmed the news.

Her name would be Ariana, meaning "gift from God."

I had waited so long! I was excited, alive with the magic of procreation, and I think Guntis fell in love with me on a whole new level. Being pregnant reminded me of the magic I had felt as a young girl in my grandfather's garden, and I carried my growing belly proudly.

As we awaited Ariana's arrival, I loved listening to Eriks' excitement about having a sister, and watching his growing sense of himself as a big brother. He imagined her with blond hair like his own, and planned to immediately teach her how to skateboard, ski, and surf. Along with Eriks, his cousins, the rest of the family and all of our friends counted the days until Ariana was born.

During labor, we discovered that Ariana was facing in the wrong direction. The doctor, not wanting to risk turning her for fear of strangling her with the umbilical cord, hoped that she would eventually turn on her own. After two days of breathing and pushing, although physically exhausted and ready for labor to be over, I was emotionally and spiritually clear.

"If I die while giving birth, it's okay," I told Guntis between contractions. "Don't be sad. I have done what I needed to do. I have owned my truth. I will have given birth to our daughter – and myself. Tell Ariana how joyful I was that she came into the world!"

Guntis was shocked by my statement, but I had come to understand that the Universe has its own agenda. I had no idea what might happen during labor. All I knew was that I was on my path, doing what I was meant to be doing. I was at peace.

On the third day of the labor process, Ariana began experiencing distress. She was taken from my womb by cesarean–section, the umbilical cord was cut, and then Guntis was holding our precious daughter next to my cheek.

Her soft beautiful face, framed with black hair, seemed familiar to me. Her dark eyes gravitated toward me as I spoke to her, welcoming her to life. Our eyes met and love flooded my body. We sank into the depths of each other's soul as if we recognized and had known each other for all eternity.

In these first few moments of her life, as Guntis cradled Ariana in his arms, I watched her melt into his heart. I knew that no father could want or love a daughter more and that Guntis was meant to be a father, not only to a son, but to a daughter as well.

I chuckled at the humor of the Universe when the nurses insisted on having a photo of this adoring father and baby enlarged and mounted permanently on the hospital nursery wall, as the ultimate expression of "fatherly love." In a flash of insight, I understood that our life journeys have less to do with what we say we want, and more to do with what we need to help us to grow. Everything that happens in our lives guides us toward wholeness.

For example, if Guntis had married a woman who did not want more children, he might never have addressed his fear, opened himself and taken this incredible risk. If I had married a man who wanted more children, I might never have learned, so precisely, so richly, how much I wanted to give birth to a child. I might never have honored my own voice. I might never have been blessed with this incredibly moving mystical experience.

During labor, lying on my back with my legs spread open, my belly raised, full, ready to split with new life, I felt one with all women throughout time who had gone through labor and given birth. In fields, tepees, caves, villages! I saw them, knew them and was one of them. I was initiated, physically, emotionally, and spiritually.

I belonged to the Clan of Womanhood.

"She softened gradually,
meeting in the light of the sun,
all the while feeling,
O, this is what it's like to be a planet
. . . and suddenly it is over
and the Universe expanded by one !"
-unknown

The celebration of Ariana's birth brought new life to

our entire family. She was loved and adored by everyone. We were amazed that within just days of her birth, she lost her black hair and grew beautiful golden locks, just like her big brother's.

My total being vibrated with love and fulfillment as I watched Eriks talk to, feed and rock Ariana to sleep. She was blessed to have such an affectionate, protective brother, and it was fitting that Ariana gave Eriks the gift of her first smile. After all, it was through mothering him that I became open to the call of Ariana's spirit.

I loved each stage of their development and wished that I could hold on to each one and not let it pass. Nothing was cuter, better, more endearing – until the next stage came along. I felt so blessed to have these two children.

Lost Babies

*B*eing so in love with mothering, it didn't surprise me that I became pregnant again seven months after Ariana was born. I was ecstatic. The Universe knew that I wanted more children, and now I knew it too! Still nursing Ariana, my body felt tired but happy.

Three months later, I had a miscarriage. Not having told anyone that I was pregnant, I mourned alone and silently. My mind became numb, but my body memorized that day, imprinting the smell of the season, the way the light fell on the colorful fall leaves and the feel of the crisp autumn air upon my aching heart.

Ten months later, at the age forty-two, I became pregnant again and rejoiced in another chance to mingle with the Gods and Goddesses. Yet again, I kept my secret close to my heart as my roller coaster cart of feelings started its pull up hill. In my eleventh week the cramping began. Wanting to believe that it could still be a normal pregnancy, I reassured myself as my cart continued up the steep track, slowly and with great effort. In a few days, I started to bleed. I pleaded. I begged. I made promises to the powers-that-be. But my cart slid down with tremendous speed and later that evening hit bottom. Another miscarriage.

My brain tried to understand what I had done wrong. Was I being punished? Was there something I should be learning? I experienced an agonizing loss, and again I mourned alone. The loss became a wound hidden deep within, where it quietly festered and burned.

Shortly before my forty-third birthday, when conception was becoming increasingly unlikely, I discovered that I was pregnant yet again. Surely this last chance would be the healthy pregnancy I longed for.

After three months of emotional ups and downs, I started to bleed. The doctor recommended bed rest. I wished that I had shared my longing to be pregnant with my family and friends so that they could offer their support, love, and hope.

On a Sunday afternoon in autumn, I rested on our living room sofa, peacefully watching the dramatic displays of reds, yellows, and oranges among the trees in the shifting light of the late afternoon sun. Without warning, a severe spasm of pain gripped my abdomen and a wave of "aloneness" washed over my body. In that instant I knew that I was no longer a "we".

I yelled for Guntis, "I've lost the baby!"

We called the emergency room. They wanted me to come in, and to bring the clots with me. I scooped them out of the toilet, and as they slipped out of my fingers, I desperately wondered which one of them was my baby! Guntis wheeled me into the emergency room, wrapped in a blanket, as I held my baby in a Ziploc bag, protected next to my belly. Unwrapping my blanket, I handed the bag to the nurse, feeling its warmth in my hands.

It was confirmed, I'd had another miscarriage. The words landed on my brain, then painfully sank deeper and deeper into my body. Leaving the hospital room, I couldn't take my eyes off the red blood clots in the white metal pan, where the nurse had emptied my Ziploc bag. How could I leave my baby in that cold pan? It didn't seem right. My heart wanted to grab the clots and bring them home with me, but my brain remained frozen.

During the following weeks, I came to understand that while my spirit might still have the energy for more babies, my body did not. My child bearing days were over.

Life continued. To my deep love for Ariana was added new gratitude and respect. If not for her feistiness and tenacity, I might never have experienced pregnancy and then birth. Those emotions extended to Eriks as well, for all the treasured moments he brought me as I loved and mothered him, for his tender heart in sharing with Ariana, prior to her birth, all his exciting stories and adventures. He most assuredly encouraged her to come into this world, and because of Eriks, I had a son. But my loss, grief, and despair floated quietly downward into my body and became buried there.

My Womb Speaks

Each passing year, as the leaves turned their gorgeous New England autumn colors, my body sensed their spectacular shades and smelled their Earthy aroma. As I felt the crisp change in the air, my heart remembered its ache. A sadness, initiated from deep within, slowly spread and filled my body until I finally recognized, consciously, the loss and the grief.

With no place to grieve, my womb shed invisible tears within my body, and in the brilliance of fall I felt as if my womb was speaking to me. It spoke to me of lost pregnancies, of miscarriages and abortions. While these are common occurrences in the lives of women, they're rarely spoken of or mourned for long.

Pregnancies that don't result in a living child are often passed over in this busy world, where results and worth are measured by products and outcomes. We move on with life, trying to forget or ignore the loss and pain. We push it deep down inside, silence our inner wails of grief and attempt to diminish any ripples on the surface.

We may want to wail with open mouths, our heads thrown back and our arms outstretched, but we don't do it. How should we mourn the unborn? Where can we bury the unnamed? What a loss not to allow ourselves to grieve, to deny our families, our friends and our communities permission to comfort us and mourn.

So it was that every fall, when mornings were crisp and leaves were brilliant, in the dying time of the year, my womb spoke to me and reminded me of the pain I still had buried. Standing among the colorful leaves, I listened to my womb. I thanked it for holding my memories and begged it not to give up on me.

Sniffing Out My Path

Several years after my third miscarriage, I saw a fuller view of my path toward wholeness. At that point, my life demonstrated the traditional measures of success. I was married, had two beautiful children and enjoyed my psychotherapy practice. We had a lovely home and many friends.

Old sorrows and injuries retreated into the shadows of time. There were no visible gaping wounds or oozing sores. Having heard and acknowledged the call of the deep feminine by having Ariana, I believed that my task was complete. I was sure I'd done all the internal work necessary to create a balanced and emotionally healthy life.

Then, one glorious day in late summer, while rushing out of a local bookstore, I noticed out of the corner of my eye some fliers on a shelf and grabbed one. It was a simple single-fold flier on blue paper. What immediately caught my eye was a totem-like drawing of several animals. What caught my soul, however, was the description of Deep Imagery:

"Deep Imagery is a unique synthesis of the Jungian Psychology concept of active imagination, the Eastern belief in chakra systems and the Native American ideology of animals as symbolic messengers of wisdom."

These words were electrifying to me, because each of these areas of interest held a special significance in my life and I had always sensed an intrinsic relationship between them.

Raised on a sheep farm during my formative years, I loved and respected animal life and the Earth. I had always felt a kinship with the Earth-centered, profound simplicity of Native American beliefs.

In the early 1970s, my exploration of Hatha and Kundalini Yoga led me to value the Eastern concept of the chakras as energy centers that govern the functioning of our bodies, and offer important information for our well-being.

During my Jungian analysis, I explored archetypal

symbols and various cultural and ethnic rites of passage. One of the books I read during that period was "The Medicine Woman" by Lynn Andrews. It tells the story of how, during her mentorship with a Native American medicine woman, she was given the task of stealing back a marriage basket from an intimidating male. I was intrigued by the parallels between her undertaking and my own Jungian transformational process of retrieving the feminine from my own daunting, masculine side.

I scanned the flier, interested in learning more about a unique imagery process blending these three traditions. Reading further, I discovered that Deep Imagery, founded and pioneered by Dr. Eligio Stephen Gallegos, uses inner images as a means of direct communication with one's own energy. Each image that spontaneously appears in a person's imagination symbolizes a part of one's energetic state. By developing a close and respectful relationship with these images through inner dialogue, a different perspective becomes clear. Old traumas and emotional wounds are healed, leading to a stronger, healthier relationship with our whole self.

During my Jungian dream work, I had often asked myself why one had to wait for a great dream to activate healing. I thought that this simple imagery technique of quieting oneself, relaxing, listening, and watching what appears in the mind's eye, could also be an effective modality for psychological and spiritual growth.

Animal images were described as being significant to this imagery work. Knowing instinctively how to be themselves, be with others and with the Earth, Dr. Gallegos believes that animals reflect a primal wisdom and that they are wise in ways that humans in this culture have forgotten.

In spite of my pressing schedule, I found myself unable to stop reading. Following this powerful "vibrational tug" at my energy, I was instinctively drawn to Deep Imagery the way an animal would sniff out its path to find its way back home again.

Usually a very cautious person, I was surprised by the urgency with which I wanted to experience Deep Imagery. Immediately upon returning home, I set up an appointment with Florence Gaia, RN, a Holistic Counselor and practitioner of Deep Imagery.

Part Two

Wild Tracks Within

*"Coming into our wholeness requires that we develop communication
and communion with all aspects of who we are. "*
- Eligios S. Gallegos, PhD.,
Discoverer of the Personal Totem Pole Process

Entering the Ark

*W*hile driving to my first session, my mind was flooded with questions and concerns. Will I be able to see these spontaneous images and animals? What if I don't see anything?

Upon meeting Florence, I was reassured by her ease and comfortable approach, and relieved to hear that there is no right or wrong way to do imagery. Florence explained that people experience images in a variety of ways. There are an infinite number of dimensions, and we meet with our animal guides not in this "here/now," but in a dimension where archetypes have their primary existence. Some people see or hear them clearly, while others may have a sense of them with no clear images at all.

During the sessions, I was to focus on each of my seven chakras, one at a time, and from each one ask an animal image to come forth. Noticing whatever image spontaneously appeared in my mind, I was to greet it respectfully and ask if it had a message for me. This dialogue would help me build a closer relationship with these animal beings and be better able to integrate all of my different energies.

The communication and relationship between the individual and their animal images appeared to be the core of the work. The role of the practitioner was to guide the individual through an initial relaxation meditation and then facilitate the dialogue between the person and his or her creature beings.

With an inner feeling of rightness, I made myself comfortable on the couch and closed my eyes. During the initial verbal meditation, Florence helped me to focus on my breath and to bring my awareness down into my body. It reminded me very much of the way I might relax during the beginning of a yoga session.

With my eyes closed, Florence asked me to bring all my attention to my crown chakra. At the top of the head and extending outward, the crown chakra relates to one's spirituality. Taking a moment to feel the energy present in my crown, I was surprised to realize that it was light, bright, almost golden.

At Florence's direction, I quietly asked inside for an animal guide to come forth. In my imagination, a lovely butterfly suddenly appeared, landing with a friendly tickle on my out-stretched finger. Her appearance drew me away from my ordinary way of being and into the magic of her world.

"Butterfly," I murmured softly, relieved that an animal had actually come to me.

Looking at Butterfly more closely, I can see that she is exquisitely patterned with luminescent colors that radiate in the light.

Florence quietly suggests that I ask Butterfly if she has a message for me. When I ask, Butterfly's appearance changes. Her wings grow huge and turn brown, like a giant moth. She becomes so large, that she fills my inner screen with her dark color. I can't distinguish Butterfly's shape in the darkness. Not understanding what is happening, I feel uneasy. At Florence's prompting, I share these feelings with Butterfly, who reappears, still brown but in her original size and with light all around her.

"You don't need to be afraid of the dark," Butterfly says kindly. "Light is needed to look at the dark." In the warmth of the light, I feel safe with Butterfly near me. As my body starts to relax, I notice that her dark brown color softens to a beautiful rich purple, and then changes from one gorgeous hue to another. Washing over the inner screen of my imagination, each color feels as if it is also washing over and softening me.

Perceiving that I am more comfortable, Butterfly flies toward me, moving so close that her wings cover my vision. Since she's transparent, however, I can see the bright light shining through from the other side. The brilliance feels magical! This loving, glowing energy of Butterfly feels very different from the heavier, darker energy of the Dark Moth she had momentarily become.

Florence suggests that I ask Butterfly about this contrast. Butterfly tells me, "There is a connection between the dark and the light!" Then Dark Moth reappears and they hover stacked, with Dark Moth on the bottom and Butterfly on top. Watching them fly together, I am less frightened of Dark Moth.

When I ask if there is anything I need to know about the light and the dark images, Butterfly responds, "Dark and Light are important aspects for you," then tenderly adds, "I will help you with the dark." I don't understand what she means or how she can help me, but trusting Butterfly, I am thankful for her kindness.

Sensing that this dialogue is complete for now, and appreciative of her warm light and gentle, colorful presence, I say good-bye. I know I will see her again and learn more from this new friend.

*****

In my next session, Florence asked me to bring my attention to my forehead chakra, situated just above and between my eyebrows. This chakra, also called "the Third

Eye," is associated with intuition and knowing.

As I focus on my forehead chakra and call forth an animal guide, I see and feel a large brown snake with diamond-patterned skin, coiled in a funnel shape on my forehead. Snake appears very powerful. Initially, I'm a little concerned about having Snake as my guide, but she is non-threatening and, to my surprise, very friendly. I have a strong sense that I can trust Snake.

When asked if there is anything that Snake wants me to know, Snake slowly turns and crawls down the side of my face. As she touches my cheek, she feels like cool satin and suddenly, I am one with Snake. From inside of Snake's head I find myself looking out through her eyes. It is fascinating! With Snake's vision, I can see great distances. My eyes are filled with a lovely landscape of green, so healthy, so lush, so beautiful!

Snake's ability to see seems to transcend time. She is the Ultimate Knower of All, seeing past, present and future in relationship to one another. As Snake, I feel as if I also have these amazing abilities. "This way of seeing is what I want to show you today," says Snake. My mind struggles to comprehend how this blending with Snake is happening. Snake tells me that I don't need to understand it, I just need to let myself be with it.

Allowing myself to flow with this imagery, I am aware of all the years that I have not been connected to this way of seeing. Having been in the mode of "doing and being busy" most of my life, I suddenly have a strong appreciation for what I have not known until right now. Humbled by this gift of her wisdom, I separate from Snake, thanking her and with great respect saying good-bye.

*****

Fascinated by what I had been experiencing, I eagerly awaited my next session, where I met my guide from the throat chakra, the area relating to my voice in the world and my ability to communicate on every level.

A little bird's beak appears and I become mesmerized by its very soft, melodious sounds. Listening, my heart feels light. I welcome Little Bird's Beak.

Hearing a lovely melody coming freely from my own throat, I realize that I have become Little Bird's Beak. The sound of my own voice astonishes me! I love singing in everyday life, yet I never thought I could carry a tune. Now, listening to my beautiful song, I laugh and enjoy my newly found ability to create a melody.

Unannounced, Dark Moth, from my first journey, flies into view, making it difficult to hear and casting a shadow over my happiness. When I express this sudden change to Florence, she suggests that I ask if there is anything I need to know about Dark Moth.

When I ask, Little Bird's Beak tells me, "It is part of you."

"What should I do when it shows up?" I asked. Little Bird's Beak says, "Sing to it. Don't be afraid of it. Love it. When you meet it with love, it, too, will lighten up."

Following this suggestion, I sing to Dark Moth, and as

42

quickly as it came, it flies away.

"Feel your power to face Moth," Little Bird's Beak encourages me. Separating from my tiny friend, I thank her for her splendid melody, her wisdom and encouragement, and watch her flutter through the trees and disappear.

*****

Next I invited an animal guide from my heart chakra, the center of love and compassion in my body, to come forth. Inexplicably, I think of a stone statue I have at home. It depicts a kneeling woman gently reaching out to feed a deer. Picturing this statue, my attention gravitates to the deer. I am quickly reminded of one of my favorite scenes from the movie "Bambi", when Bambi meets Skunk for the first time.

Seeing sweet Skunk pop her head out from underneath a patch of flowers, a sense of peaceful, loving oneness with all creatures and plants fills my body. I am at home!

I assume that Bambi is my animal guide for my heart chakra, but as I look directly at him, he begins to fade away. Skunk glances over at me with a twinkle in her eye, and suddenly, it is clear that Skunk is my heart chakra guide!

Laughing out loud, I am surprised but delighted. For some reason it seems so right having Skunk in my heart. I sense that I already know her. So soft and strong, Skunk is very simple, innocent, loving, and open to others. Yet she makes no bones about being a skunk and protecting her-self when necessary. I love little Skunk and tell her so. She smiles, rather shyly. Skunk carries a simple, uncomplicated message.

"To love is so easy," she says. "Just be yourself." Smiling sweetly, Skunk says good-bye and slips under the flowers, leaving me with a joyful heart.

*****

Curious about what other animals might be waiting inside of me, I was excited about my next session, where I would meet my solar plexus chakra guide. This area, at the base of my rib cage, relates to my will and to my power to act clearly, decisively, and effectively.

The energy here feels very still, but incredibly strong. Calling forth an animal guide, I am astounded to see a massive brown buffalo head emerge directly from my solar plexus. Buffalo's large flat forehead is wider than my chest. I can feel and smell the Earthy warmth of his thick brown fur, as it brushes against my nose. I see the kind strength in his large brown eyes.

With each breath I take, I have a growing awareness of Buffalo's tremendous size and solidness. His broad head spreads my ribs, making space and allowing more of his great body to emerge. With this expansion, my breathing becomes less labored. My ribs curve around the sides of Buffalo's head, while the rest of my upper body serves as a head dress for him. It is apparent that Buffalo is my support.

Buffalo invites me to become one with him. I see my

legs and feet entering Buffalo's legs and hooves. My body is Buffalo's body. I am dense and sturdy. I stand firmly rooted to the Earth, yet I know I can move with speed should the need arise. Buffalo feels familiar to me, as if we have long been together.

Buffalo knows exactly how to be and what to do. His relationship with himself, with other buffalos and with the Earth seems uncomplicated. As Buffalo, in right-relationship with the Earth, I graze tranquilly on the grass. With an innate wisdom, after I eat a little grass, I move on and eat a little more in a different area.

I thank Buffalo for coming and for showing me his immense and solid strength.

As my awareness of his presence fades, my ribs and solar plexus remain open and expanded. I have a sense of my own solid power that I've never known before.

*****

In my next session, after barely completing the beginning relaxation, my belly or stomach chakra, just below my naval, the center of feelings, emotions and passion, demanded my attention.

Quickly bounding out of my stomach, a huge brown bear with mighty arms, reaches out to touch me, as if he has been waiting eagerly for me. Bear is so vivacious! His arms are open to embrace me and the whole world. I am so excited by his enthusiasm and laughter that I love him immediately! I ask Bear if he has a message for me.

45

"I am part of a living, awakening spirit," Bear tells me. Instantly I find myself becoming one with Bear. A tingling sensation fills my whole body with joyfulness. My arms are passionately powerful and open. While this energy feels familiar to me, I am surprised by its force and urgency.

Walking around, enjoying Bear's vibrancy, I tell him with excitement, "I feel so intensely alive!" Bear takes pleasure in my enthusiasm, then he instructs me, "Feel this energy, respect it and honor it. It's yours to use."

When it is time to separate, I hate to leave Bear's body. Assured by Bear that he will be with me whenever I think of him, I depart, thanking him for sharing this exhilarating energy. Saying good-bye, I hug him with my big arms, telling him, "I love you. I will never forget you." A whole new part of me has come to life!

*****

I met my last animal guide at the root or grounding chakra, located at the base of the spine. Its function relates to one's relationship or connection with the Earth, and also one's sense of security, or grounding in life.

The energy in this area feels heavy and compressed. Asking for an animal guide to come forth, I see dense green moss. Looking closer, I notice tiny bugs living on its surface. Underneath the thick moss, I see layers of moist brown Earth. Further down still, buried in the rich soil, I see an ancient nautilus shell, which I realize is my root animal guide. She too has been waiting for me to communicate with her.

She rests quietly in the darkness under the Earth, as if she is a part of it. She has been here for thousands of years. Nautilus Shell is like a buried pearl—she is beyond color. It is with great awe that I sense she is "The Mother."

I ask Mother Nautilus Shell if she has a message for me, and she says, "You don't have to be afraid of the dark, for I am in the dark." My surprise at her mention of the dark is overshadowed by my pressing need to become one with her. Blending with Mother Nautilus Shell has a peaceful, timeless quality. She has endless strength and the ability to live in both dark and light. Mother Nautilus Shell is quiet, yet abundantly alive. She tells me, "I am your link to the Earth and your ancestors."

Her ancient love for me and her hallowed connection to the Earth flood my body. I thank Mother Nautilus Shell for sharing her eternal gifts. Revering her ancient sacredness, words cannot express how honored I am to have her as my guide.

*****

Several days after that last session, while driving home from work along a winding country road, passing by a farm, I saw a magnificent black horse standing in a fenced-in field. I stopped my car at the side of the road, and with a new level of understanding, sat peacefully and watched this horse.

His nostrils flair and his breath swirls and rises in the

crisp air. His eyes are like dark liquid pools, inviting me to swim with his spirit. I experience a deep bond with this horse. I feel his amazing energy and tremendous power in my body, as if they were mine. My body moves as he moves. This unexpected union takes my breath away!

My perception of and relationship with animals has been forever changed from my journeys with Deep Imagery. I finally know deep within that we are all connected on this Earth. Whatever happens to any animal on this planet happens to me also. With the unassailable integrity of experience, with not just my intellect, but with my whole body, I comprehend the true meaning of "being One with."

Loving My Majestic Being of Hate

Several times during the sessions with my chakra animals, they made reference to the aspects of Dark and Light. I decided that I wanted to experience these opposing energies or polarities in my next session of Deep Imagery.

After my relaxation meditation, I asked inside myself which polarity I was to work with first. Unexpectedly, my animals made it clear that I was to encounter not my animal guides of dark and light, but my guides of love and hate.

It fascinated me that my animal guides had their own ideas about what needed to happen and I trusted their judgment. I asked which animal guide—love or hate—I needed to meet initially.

A beautiful deer appears and I know it is my animal of love. I watch as Deer changes form in my mind's eye from a young fawn, to a buck and then a doe. Not understanding the significance of these changes, yet welcoming Deer, I ask her what I need to learn.

Deer tells me, "You can be gentle and still be strong." I see her strong legs and neck, and in contrast, I feel her gentle spirit. I enjoy watching Deer bound gracefully through the woods.

"Listen to your heart, the birds, and the air," Deer states kindly. "Your heart desires to be free. Let it fly and dance with the birds among the trees." My heart follows her lead, and Deer and I prance through the forest, laughing.

Breathless, stopping to rest, Deer tells me that she is hungry. As I stretch out my hand to feed her, Deer starts to grow larger. Again her form changes from female to male and quickly back to female. Yearning for Deer to remain female, I feel conflicted. Strangely, I believe it would be easier for me to feel closer to Deer in the male form. Although I recognize that these feelings are significant, I am unclear why.

Understanding my struggle and my need, Deer remains in her female form. I ask Deer if there is anything I need to know about this confusion. Deer smiles and instruct me to touch her. Moving closer to Deer, placing my arms around her muscular neck, I feel the warm comfort of her body. As my fingers glide over her smooth coat, I sense her love for me, and any ambivalence about her being female disappears. Empowered by her feminine strength and grace, I know I am capable of accomplishing anything. I thank her for her patience.

My animal guide of hate waits for me, and I am apprehensive. Asking it to come forth, I see total darkness. Uneasy, I think that my animal guide of hate must be a terrible monster hiding in the dark.

Suddenly, in a shaft of nearly blinding light, I see the shape of four legs and a tail. Watching this luminous image, the awareness comes to me that this animal does not wish to scare me. As I slowly release my fear of meeting this creature, the image becomes more visible.

I see white fur, and I'm astonished that my animal of hate is not dark and evil. As the animal lifts its head, I see it is a White Wolf, stunning and majestic. Its pure white fur glistens in the light. White Wolf is female. She is not bad or hurtful, and in fact, I sense that White Wolf is linked to the Divine. She signals me to come closer and to smell her fur. Burying my nose in her thick coat, I am reminded of the smell of the Earth, and a pleasurable warmth travels throughout my body. Silently, I question how this could be hate. It is not dark!

Finally, I ask, "Are you my animal of hate?"

White Wolf answers, "It is all in how you see it. When I am in the woods, out of sight or hidden in the dark, I am hate or anger. Out of the shadows, I am love and light. Embrace hate and anger, for they are merely other aspects of you."

Deer, who has been standing patiently at my side approves, lovingly licking my cheek. I ask the two animals, Deer of love and White Wolf of hate to meet. Approaching each other, it is clear that they know and respect each other and are comfortable together.

I question whether it would be appropriate for these two animals to become one. Immediately, Deer and White Wolf blend together, transforming into an exquisite bald eagle.

"Come join us as we fly, and you will see that united we are most powerful," Eagle says.

Climbing onto Eagle's sturdy back, I clutch its commanding wings. Soaring together, I am aware of how very steady and balanced Eagle feels and how luminously alive I feel. We glide through the brilliant sky. Then, landing on a large rock outcrop for me to dismount, Eagle spreads its regal wings and flies away.

Playing a significant role in the balancing and healing of my energies, this polarity journey and the timing of it encouraged me to turn off my rational, thinking mind, relinquish control, and to trust that my animal guides know exactly what needs to happen and when.

Skillfully creative, Deer and White Wolf taught me to integrate aspects of my life that I might not have otherwise recognized as essential for my healing. Broadening and redefining my understanding of hate and anger, Deer and

White Wolf invited these feelings into the light, creating a loving acceptance where once lived fear and shame.

Equally important was the gentle manner in which they assisted me to transform my perception of the female essence. Understanding my ease with the masculine-oriented world, Deer and White Wolf patiently guided me to become more comfortable with the feminine. Demonstrating strength, yet gentleness, using the senses of touch, smell, and vision, they helped me to re-align with the feminine knowing, through my body rather than my intellect. As I opened to vulnerability and trust, old wounds began to heal.

Deer and White Wolf reminded me of my natural link to the Earth, powerfully laying the fertile groundwork for all of my future journeys and connections with the feminine.

A Place of Belonging

In Greek mythology, Procrustes, the ancient champion of enforced conformity, was said to have placed a bed on the road to Athens, upon which every passer-by must lie down and be measured. Athens, the center of culture and achievement at that time, symbolically represents accomplishment and success. According to the legend, travelers had to fit perfectly on Procrustes' bed in order to continue on their way. In other words, this bed depicted "the standard." Anyone too tall or wide would be cut to fit. Anyone too short would be stretched.

A similar process happens to us in society today. As children, we learn that some of our feelings, desires, abilities, even dreams may not be acceptable to our family or the culture in which we are raised. Needing love and approval, we learn to discard or deny these parts of ourselves. We're taught that our parents, teachers and other authority figures know better than we do what is best for us. As a result, we often forsake our uniqueness and try to adjust to the standards, expectations, and demands of others.

These abandoned parts often remain hidden even from ourselves. We bury them alive. If they remain buried, they become wounds in our souls. The identity we recognize and acknowledge is almost certainly not who we truly are. We survive. We may even be very successful as measured by the cultural expectations we grew up with. But these are the "lives of quiet desperation."

Having buried and forgotten essential elements of ourselves as individuals, we cannot be our true, vibrant selves. In order to be all that we are capable of being, we must return to the past and gather up all of our discarded abilities, dreams and energies. Once we bring them into our present, acknowledge and honor them, we can then remember and recreate our true identities.

In Deep Imagery, the meeting together all of one's energies or chakra animal guides is called a "Council." Each person's crown chakra guide determines when to hold a council. If the time is not right, the crown chakra guide indicates what is needed first. If the time is right, all the chakra animals together determine the agenda of the meeting and how to work together for the individual's growth and well being.

The purpose of the council is to allow those energies to flow together more freely, more in balance. Following a council, people report feeling more peaceful and centered, more in harmony in their lives. The council acts much like a circle of elders, watching over, supporting and guiding the tribe.

Some animals may already know each other and work well together. Others may meet for the first time, and sometimes resolution of conflicts is required. Each council meeting is unique, depending entirely upon what healing is required.

Before my first council began, I greeted each of my chakra animals:

Butterfly: crown (spirituality)
Snake: forehead (knowing/intuition)
Bird's Beak: throat (voice/communication)
Skunk: heart (love/compassion)
Buffalo: solar plexus (will/personal power)
Big Brown Bear: belly (feelings/emotions)
Mother Nautilus Shell: root (grounding/survival)

In spite of all the amazing messages and gifts my animal guides had offered me, nothing could prepare me for the intense experience and astonishing healing of my first council.

At first barely noticeable and then stronger, a swirling sensation began in my body. All my energy began to move forcefully in a circular motion and I instinctively grabbed for support. There was a momentary sensation of falling, and then the ground of my being felt solid and stable. My chest and abdomen expanded and my body vibrated with life. I could feel and see all of my chakra animals in their various locations in my body.

Snake slips down from my forehead and glides around Little Bird's Beak. For a second, I am apprehensive about their encounter, but watch quietly. Snake continues slowly crawling down my body to meet the other animals. Butterfly, my crown animal flutters around me. Skunk smiles and nods as Buffalo emerges from under my ribs. I am aware of Mother Nautilus Shell's quiet approval.

I see and feel Bear as he emerges powerfully half way out of my stomach. Bear turns, extending his large arms, signaling the formation of a circle, which the animals form on top of my body. Bear has a very important place among the animals, as his all-encompassing massive arms hold the circle. However, it is evident that each animal guide is important in its own unique way. They love and respect each other and work well together.

As the circle is forming I begin to hear music, a song which starts with the soft sound of each animal's breath and crescendos into a thrilling choir of their distinctive tones. Their song and movement resound in my body with a sacred oneness. They tell me, "This is the Sound of Life. It's living!"

Gently moving in a circular motion, slowly increasing their speed, my animals create a tingling liveliness which spreads throughout my body. Around and around, faster and faster they move, producing heat with their movement. The animals start to move so quickly that they become a blur of color to my eyes, turning into a golden, honey-like liquid. Spiraling up and down, the warm amber fluid forms the shape of an inverted funnel, with the large round top resting on my out-stretched body. This whirling funnel becomes a vortex as the sounds and golden light blend, filling and lifting me as it circles. We travel, first as separate individuals and then as a single being, up through the bright light, spiraling around and back down, flooding my body with a brilliant radiance. Held by my animals, I am aware of my bond with them and of my direct link to the Universe. I am, at one and the same time, separate and a part of the Whole, filled with complete love and peace. Then all my animals, in the form of intense golden nectar, pour directly into my heart, setting it ablaze with their magnitude.

"You are full of Heartspirit," they murmur. "Your heart is golden." Slowly returning to their rightful places in my body, my animals whisper with the deepest affection, "You belong with us." My eyes fill with tears as I hear myself say, "I've been searching so long." Their voices continue, echoing in loving song, "You have a place with us. You have a place . . . forever."

At the end of this council, leaving my animals, with their unconditional love and acceptance, and returning to my normal state of mind took a long time. My brain, with its usual running list of things to do, was unavailable to me, as if it had tripped a switch and turned itself off. Organizing one thought in front of another, even moving my body, was difficult. When my mind finally rejoined my body, I began to understand the tremendous impact of this council. I was aware that together my animals had created a beneficial symbiosis, an essence of love and warmth that was greater than the sum of the individual parts.

To this day, my animals are my centering vessel. They fill me with their infinite love and their words, "You have a place with us. You have a place forever," vibrate within my heart and body -- the eternal song of life!

Wolf Mother

*M*y chakra animals' deep love and acceptance, so
obvious during the council, as well as my own shifting perspective of the feminine helped to prepare me for the next
major journey in my healing. My animals decided I was to
meet with the polarities of light and dark. Remembering
that in my first session, both my crown and root animals
had offered to help me with my fear of the dark, I became
curious about what they meant by "fear of the dark".

Focusing on my breath, I brought my awareness

inward and asked an animal guide of the light to come forth. Immediately, a beautiful white owl made a grand entrance.

Owl is downy soft and has deep dark eyes. I'm drawn to her beauty and quiet presence. Owl wants me to sit in stillness and observe her.

Owl tells me, "When you are quiet, you become aware of many feelings."

As my body and mind quiet, four paws, barely discernable in the dark, come into focus. I sense that these paws belong to my animal of the dark, and that the time has arrived for me to meet this guide.

Very slowly the image becomes more visible. I begin to see a bushy tail and I know it is a wolf. Wolf's body remains invisible, but I sense its presence, and feel my body tense in anxiety. Responding to my discomfort, Wolf moves away from me, becoming much smaller and lighter, appearing more like a white marble, museum statue. I am strangely relieved.

I watch as Wolf changes into the Roman mythological Wolf Mother, who cared for and nursed the abandoned twins, Romulus and Remus, who later were said to be the founders of Rome. I see Wolf Mother standing with her teats hanging down, as the two infants suckle on the ground and I am mesmerized.

Gradually, Wolf Mother and her infants become larger, moving closer to me. As they do, a wave of vulnerability engulfs my body. Somehow I sense that it is painful to be this mother wolf, with her connection to the Earth and to all that is natural. Watching Wolf Mother nursing her babies, I am aware of how distant I have become from nature and all that is natural. Totally captivated by Wolf Mother's presence, I feel that right here is exactly where I need to be.

Wolf Mother steps toward me and, as she does, a deep ache pierces my chest and I experience an odd sense of separation from my body. Very slowly, I am drawn closer and closer to Wolf Mother, until finally I become Wolf Mother. Surprisingly, I feel at home in her body. I have the overwhelming sensation of wondering where I have been all this time. This connection with Wolf Mother feels absolutely right, as if I have come back to my true body!

My eyes survey my strong, furry arms. I feel their gentle strength and power. Glancing further down my wolf body, I see that I am lying down and six giant teats, covering my chest and stomach, are filled with milk. I am amazed by the presence of these mounds of nurturing flesh.

Wolf Mother encourages me to feel her "wolfness." Experiencing myself physically as Wolf Mother, a raw sorrow wells up from within. She says, "It is okay to feel your sadness and bring it out into the light." Wolf Mother's words pierce my heart, and grief quickly rises up from within my body and spills out of my eyes. With an agonizing gasp of recognition, I know that this anguish relates to my past abortions. This over-whelming sorrow takes my mind by surprise, because not only have I worked on this issue in traditional therapy, I have always believed in a woman's right to choose. Yet, in the moment, my body is undeniably overflowing with deep loss.

"You need to pay attention to what is going on inside your body, because this is where you will find your grounding," Wolf Mother lovingly tells me. Listening to her words, my eyes slowly and purposefully scan my wolf body, and I become aware of three small wolf babies on my stomach. Instantly, I feel a maternal bond with them, needing to help each of the precious wolf babies find a breast. My heart aches. Tears literally stream down my face. I know that these babies represent the three babies I had aborted.

Anguished, I tell them, "I am so sorry I was not able to bring you into life." Watching them suckle, I sadly realize that I was out of touch with my body. And for the first time, I wrap my arms around my babies.

Something stirs in my abdomen, and three more beautiful wolf babies appear on my stomach! I know these represent the three babies I had miscarried. My belly is covered with an abundance of life. I am grief stricken, yet my heart is filled with deep joy and connection. "I am finally whole again. I feel like I have a whole litter," I say, sharing my delighted heart with Wolf Mother.

"I am the Mother," I whisper, and I feel her agree as she gazes deep into my eyes and heart. With love and gratitude, I thank Wolf Mother, who softly tells me, "This is why I have come."

When I ask both Owl, my animal of light and Wolf Mother, my animal of dark, if they would be willing to meet, Owl swoops in, giving six melodious hooting sounds, one for each of the lost babies. I know she has waited patiently and for a long time to sing her healing song for me. As Owl sings her lullaby, I feel my wet nipples exposed to the air and my breasts become full again.

Gently, Owl flies into Wolf Mother's body and the two merge. Wolf Mother's front paws become big white wings, while her head remains part owl and part wolf. She has six big full teats on her abdomen. Her wolf tail falls below her splendid broad wings, as she begins to ascend in the sky.

I am separate, and at the same time, I am also them. Soaring as one, I feel gloriously alive as I observe the round, vivid green of Mother Earth passing below. Over the tips of our wings, I see a beautiful bright green field, newly planted and sprouting with fresh growth. "Yes, it is new life," they say warmly. "We are celebrating new life in your heart."

As we glide in the lovely azure sky, I see three puffy, pure-white feathers hanging from each large wing. Elated, I understand that these six small white feathers symbolize my six babies, now free to fly.

Grateful for Owl's patient lesson of serene stillness and Wolf's intuitive wisdom about my fears, I left this journey with a whole new appreciation for the intricate and undeniable healing potential of Deep Imagery.

Allowing me to move at my own pace, Wolf Mother's gentle approach offered me the time I needed to re-identify with my body on both a physical and an emotional level. Lending me her body and mirroring my pain, Wolf Mother guided me to uncover feelings that waited to be released. Rooted in her own strength, carrying for me the image of the Great Mother or archetypal feminine, Wolf Mother listened to and witnessed my grief without judgment. Aiding me to bring important pieces of myself into the light, she freed me to be reunited with my lost babies.

My Friend Turtle

I felt impelled to meet the man who pioneered and teaches Deep Imagery. Then, in one of those magical, serendipitous occurrences, I ran across a brochure regarding him. Dr. Eligio Stephen Gallegos was offering a weekend workshop near my home, and I registered. The workshop took place in the spring of 1995, and about twenty people attended. During the weekend, we were scheduled to meet our seven chakra animal guides and experience a council meeting.

Having just returned from a week-long women's retreat with Dr. Jean Shinoda Bolen, the door to my soul was ajar. Aware of the powerful experiences I had already had with Deep Imagery, I was curious and open. However, I could never have guessed that I'd be propelled into a journey of love, life, acceptance and mystery that would continue to unfold for years.

After introducing himself, Dr. Gallegos (who called himself Steve) shared a bit of his personal history and the miraculous story of what led him to Deep Imagery. Steve set a comfortable, easy tone in the group. As I heard his kind voice say, "Humans are the story-telling animals," it sounded familiar, almost like a soothing mantra I had heard hundreds of times before. Hearing him speak about Deep Imagery and its profound effect on people's lives, I understood that he was re-teaching us how to hear our own living myths.

After relaxing the group with a verbal meditation, Steve began by having us close our eyes and picture a seed, the essence of new growth and life. We were to communicate silently with this seed to learn what it needed in order to grow. Then, opening our eyes, we shared our seed journeys with the group. He explained that by sharing our journeys and witnessing the stories of others, our own experience would deepen.

My seed was an acorn, which I planted in the Earth. It grew quickly, magically into a solid oak tree. I watched the leaves open and the tree become very large and full. I watched seasons pass, leaves growing, turning red-brown and falling to leave the branches bare. I saw that from this oak, many small trees sprouted up around it. As years passed, these trees continued to grow and spread.

After everyone had shared, we closed our eyes again to meet our chakra animal guides. I was excited and curious to see whether my same old friends would appear or whether I would meet new ones. We began by asking for an animal guide from our heart chakra to come forth.

Skunk appears, and I am delighted to see this endearing little creature again. Skunk is standing on the edge of my heart looking down into it, as if it were a deep well. Skunk is accompanied by his friend Ready Fox. I welcome them, then peer with them into the well.

Skunk says, "We need to stretch your heart!" They gently pull the sides of my heart, making it wider. Deciding more light is needed, Skunk shines a huge stage flood light on my heart, warming and softening it. As I watch, both laughing and amazed at the playful silliness of it, Skunk and Ready Fox fluff up my heart like a feather pillow. Nestling comfortably into it, appearing quite pleased with himself, Skunk sighs and says, "Now...." He seems to have completed his task, and knows that my heart is now ready for whatever happens next. I thank Skunk and Fox for their help and bid them farewell.

Next, I focus on my throat and ask to meet an animal from my throat chakra.

A frog appears on my right collarbone. This new animal surprises me, as previously, my guide for this chakra had been Little Bird's Beak.

Noting the frog sitting comfortably on my collarbone, I remember with amusement that my mother had collected ceramic frogs. I am both pleased and curious to speak with Frog. I sense that this frog is very wise and knowing and greet him respectfully. Frog says, "I have brought a friend for you to meet," and directs my attention to Turtle, who suddenly appears right beside him on my collarbone.

I'm instantly apprehensive. The apprehension turns to panic as I am confronted with my life-long fear of turtles. My first instinct is to run right out of the workshop. My body reacts with revulsion. Finally daring to look, I see the skin on Turtle's neck stretch and hang as he turns his head. I notice the claws on his feet and see his eyes blink and re-blink as he looks around. I smell the dank smell of turtle and shivers of old terror run up and down my spine.

I have already dealt with my fear of turtles in traditional psychotherapy, by desensitizing myself and by approaching the fear rationally. "You can't just get up and run out of the workshop!" my mind says. But my body does not care about what I can and cannot do. Terror sweeps from my stomach up to my throat and sticks there like a knot. I feel Turtle on my body and I cannot get away. I'm choking!

Finally, I speak up and tell Frog, "I don't want Turtle on my body!" Hearing these words, it strikes me that in real life I have always had this particular fear of turtles -- the fear of turtles on my body. I remember that as a child, I had two small pet turtles which crawled out of their bowl and became lost in our house, never to be found. A highly

70

imaginative child, I had nightmares that the lost turtles found their way onto my bed, entered my body through my eye sockets and crawled around inside me.

Suddenly, I am reliving this nightmare! The turtles have entered my body and I can see the bumps of their shells and feel my skin lift as they crawl across my forehead.

My body feels hot and I have the urge to throw up. Just as quickly, my body feels cold and filled with terror. I need to run, to get away from the turtles, but they are inside my skin and there is no place to go! I am trapped.

At the peak of my fright, I hear a soft, calm voice from within say, "Stop running. Face this fear, face these feelings." Then, silence. Weary, wanting to be free from this terror, and somehow feeling less alone after the sound of the calm voice, I hear myself numbly whisper, "Okay."

With the hopes of gaining some courage, I take a deep breath. Challenging Turtle, I say, "Okay! Come on Turtle! Crawl all over my whole body if you want to!"

Bracing myself, a stone cold calmness washes over me as I try to separate from my body. I feel turtles crawling all over me! My body stiffens. I turn my face away. I can barely breathe!

Instantly, the memory of a childhood sexual trauma floods my body. I am frozen in this experience, as all the feelings I had at that time come rushing back to me. I feel the same tremendous fear. I feel the shame. I feel that I have done something bad. Recalling the incident, which had been buried in the shadows of my memory, I begin to sob. My body trembles uncontrollably, both from this

71

memory and from the release of all the energy that has kept it hidden.

Between the sobs and gasps for breath, my childhood feelings spew forth like projectile vomit. I feel that I am bad. I can't do things right. I am no good. I see myself five years old, when after feeding Quackie our family duck, I accidentally left the pen door open and a fox ate him. The next morning, when I entered Quackie's cage to feed him, I saw a pile of feathers and bones beside his food dish. Fearful and horrified, I knew it was my fault and I was ashamed.

Next, I see flashes of myself several years later, when I was given a chameleon as a pet. I hated touching the maggot-like worms he ate and I could not stand to feed him. I wanted him to die.

Intertwined with these rapid-fire childhood flashes and all my associated feelings are the memories and visual images of my three miscarriages and three abortions. My body is gripped with the horror of my failure, of not being able to keep things alive! I sob desperately.

Steve Gallegos, with the other members of the group waiting, allows room for all my feelings, as if knowing they have been waiting to come forth, needing to be voiced and witnessed. When my body is exhausted and emptied of grief and fear, Steve gently asks me if I would be willing to ask Turtle what needs to happen for me to heal. Asking Turtle, I see an image of a vagina. The vagina is slowly being stretched. The top of a head begins to crown, as if a birth is taking place. Then two pure white doves fly out of the vagina.

One dove lands on my right shoulder and the other on my left. I feel my shoulders being gently pulled back and my stature straightened. The Doves tell me, "You didn't do anything wrong. You don't need to carry shame any more. You can walk tall and walk with pride."

Immediately, a great sense of warmth, love, and acceptance begins to spread throughout my body. A weight from inside, that I did not realize I had been carrying, lifts. Peace and gratitude fill my heart as light shines from within me. I stand a proud, tall female with a beautiful, pure white dove on each shoulder.

Feeling as if I have been given a remarkable treasure, I thank Turtle for both his enduring love and kindness and for carrying all that pain and sorrow for me these many years.

Returning home from the workshop, I am exhausted, but I have a new awareness of my body. Fragments of my journeys and feelings from the weekend drift through me in a physical sense, as if my body is communicating with me.

My body definitely feels taller and thinner, almost stretched. I sense, not only with my mind, but with my entire being that my perspective has expanded. I see things from a higher, more extended view, almost as if I were a tree that has quickly grown stronger and taller.

While sharing the events of the workshop with Guntis, I rubbed my collarbone and noticed that it felt sensitive. Suddenly, an image of a childhood event flashed into my mind. An uninvolved spectator, I watched, and later I wrote:

"I am two years old. It is early morning, and my mother is away. I fall from the couch, breaking both collarbones. My grandmother, who is caring for me, doesn't realize what has happened. I see myself in a hospital that same evening, with five tall people in white jackets holding me down!" Years later I learned that the doctors had told my mother they needed to re-break my collarbones and set them properly, but for some reason they could not use anesthetic. Trusting the medical advice, as parents did in those days, my mother agreed.

What power this Deep Imagery has to connect me so exquisitely with my body!

I have a new awareness and respect for my body, and honor it for all it has endured, for the pain it has suffered, absorbed and accepted and for its ability to keep on going.

Part Three

Coming Home to My Soul

"If you travel far enough, one day, you will recognize yourself coming down the road to meet yourself. And you will say – YES."
— *Marion Woodman*

Stripped of All My Regalia

*D*uring the weekend workshop, as emotionally difficult as it was reliving trauma from my childhood, my soul was ignited in a way it had not been since my daughter's conception and birth. I knew I needed to be trained in this powerful and transformative imagery work. Steve told me that the next training would take place the following month in Ireland. Although I never imagined traveling so far, I called Ireland for information about the training and was told that, due to a recent withdrawal, there was one space left. I knew it was meant for me.

From the moment I boarded the airplane and heard Irish accents, a surprising warmth spread through my body. Touching an unknown place inside of me, the lilting sounds were somehow familiar and comforting. Landing in Shannon, I was delighted to see that the patchwork of green fields rolled right down to the sea!

On the first day of the training, I walked into a lovely little white-washed, thatched-roofed cottage on the edge of Galway Bay. The setting was perfect. The smell of peat permeated the air as it burned in the fireplace. The living room was small, cozy and warm, with two couches, a chair, and a number of pillows strewn on the rug. The door remained open, offering a view of the glistening sea, as it rolled ever so slowly closer and closer to the cottage.

Sitting on the couch and looking around at the fireplace, books, and curtains, I felt as if I had been there before. It made no sense intellectually, but my body recognized the place. My chest vibrated and my body responded to the energy in the room.

I watched as the other twelve women, mostly Irish, arrived and took places in the circle. Their easy, friendly greetings were animated with laughter, and I was excited. My whole body, my whole being, knew I had come to the right place.

At dinner, someone asked what we would learn during the *second* week of training. Shocked, because I had no idea that there would be a second week, I asked about it and was told that week two was set for the fall. There would also be two more two-week training sessions during the following two years.

I also learned that since the cottage was too small to accommodate all of us overnight, I would be sleeping at a local bed and breakfast, a short drive away. I didn't have a rental car, and knew that even if I did, I wouldn't be able to drive on the narrow windy roads on what felt like the wrong side of the street!

Realizing that I would have to rely upon other people, I started to feel uncomfortable. And what about my caffeine addiction to diet cola? I was greatly relieved to see that they had diet sodas in Ireland, but how would I replenish my supply? I started to feel desperate, hating to have to depend upon anyone.

Although the women's Irish brogues were delightfully rhythmical and I loved hearing the sound of them, they unsettled my analytical mind. I wished that I could better understand what they were saying. They were speaking English, yet, I couldn't decipher words, expressions, even whole paragraphs. They spoke so quickly! I had always relied on my ability to communicate with people in a clear articulate manner, but in this situation I was at a loss.

When it was raining and the women spoke of "wellies," I wondered what they meant. Then I watched as they pulled on their traditional tall green Irish boots, and surmised that these boots must be wellies.

The women referred to the day as a "soft day" and I pondered what that meant. Walking outside during the break, unable to see any rain, but feeling an almost invisible mist washing against my face, I understood perfectly.

Being in a foreign land with a different culture, my analytical mind had to take a back seat. I had to settle for getting the gist of things and feeling the tone of what someone was saying, rather than understanding the actual words. Having left at home my identity as wife, mother and psychotherapist, I was in an unfamiliar country on many levels, without a car and knowing no one. I was stripped of all my supports and defenses, my persona, even my language.

Again I was reminded of Inanna's descent into the underworld. Remembering that she had one piece of her magnificent regalia removed at each of the seven gates, I realized that I, too, had already had several exquisitely woven, protective shawls removed from me.

On the first night of the training, snuggling down in bed under my blanket of Irish wool, I reviewed the remarkable day filled with new experiences, sights and sounds. I was both excited and anxious. How would I make it through the whole week? I was homesick already. Tossing and turning, I finally surrendered to sleep, and dreamed.

In my dream, I'm in a huge, old, abandoned building. I am running and breathless. Aliens are after me, and they'll kill me if they catch me. With one hand, I am clutching a baby girl against my chest. The building is falling apart and many of the floor boards are missing, making walking dangerous and running almost out of the question!

I am desperately trying to discover a way out, but I'm on the second floor. There is an exit, but it requires walking across a plank two stories up with nothing underneath it but empty space!

I am afraid of heights and I hear my shallow, quick breath and feel my whole body fill with fear. The plank looks wobbly and unsafe. There are others behind me, also trying to get out. They're waiting for me to cross the plank, and I'm afraid they may push me in their desire to escape.

The man behind me is patient and kind. Without saying anything, holding the others back, he gives me all the time I need to cross the plank. Offered the opportunity to move in my own time, without being pushed or rushed, my confidence builds and I am very grateful to him. Drumming up every bit of courage I have, I cross the plank. Taking a deep breath, I am free.

Suddenly horrified, I realize that during my rush to make it out alive, I have forgotten my little girl! I have abandoned her in the building. How could I have done that? Did she fall out of my arms? What is wrong with me? Terrified, I know that I have to go back into the building to find and rescue my little girl.

Waking early in the morning, I reviewed my dream. I knew that it symbolized what I had to do in my life: I had to go back and rescue the little girl inside of me.

The baby girl also represented my children's children - the future. As we change and rescue ourselves, by healing our past, we also affect the next generation by breaking unhealthy patterns.

I had a sense that this dream represented how Deep Imagery could help each of us to go back, collect the lost pieces and rescue the forgotten child within each of us.

In this lovely little spot in Ireland, far from all I knew and all that knew me, I began to learn more about this amazingly simple and sublime process of Deep Imagery. Sitting in a circle later in the morning, Steve shared more about his personal experiences with the imagery work and demonstrated the guidelines for facilitating others in their journeys with their animal guides. He explained that we would learn this skill by journeying, by practicing facilitating others in the group and by sharing our experiences and relevant feelings in the morning circle.

First we were to meet a seed, the essence of potential new life, and a guide for what needed to happen for our own growth. Once the seed appeared in our imagination, we would welcome it and begin to communicate with it, listening for any messages and asking what it needed to flourish.

As we started, I called inwardly for a seed to come forth. A seed appeared with a large, round, red root. Studying this root, it becomes clear that it is a beet -- a big, red juicy beet! I welcome it and ask if it has a message for me.

"My flesh is full of the red blood of life – soul blood," Beet says with great contentment. Beet wants me to take a big bite of it. Although I think it a strange request, I agree. Biting into Beet as I would an apple, I expect it to be hard. Instead, Beet's flesh is pleasantly soft and delicious. With my second bite, the bright red beet juice splatters all over my face. I want to wipe the juice off my face, to be neat and "presentable," but Beet stops me.

"Do not wipe your face," Beet tells me firmly, then chuckles with satisfaction and continues, "Bathe in this red juice! Let it flow and enjoy it. Let this red blood cover you and bring you back to life!" I sense that Beet knows me very well and enjoys our relationship. It feels wonderful to be known, accepted and loved by Beet. Taking another bite, I allow the red juice to run down my face. We laugh together as it drips off my chin.

Sensing that this session, although very short, is complete for now, I thank Beet for his sense of humor and his caring message and say good-bye.

After this journey, I asked myself, "Am I not fully alive? Has there been a quiet hemorrhaging of my soul?"

In her book, *Women Who Run with the Wolves,* Clarissa Pinkola Estes recounts a story called 'Seal Skin Soul Skin.' This story teaches that when we are not true to ourselves, not living in our own skin, we start to dry out, wither and age. It becomes difficult to breathe and we may even begin to die. Was that happening to me?

I trusted Beet and somehow what he said rang true. I sensed that Beet, like all my animal and other guides, would lead me step by step toward wholeness.

The Spirit of Bear

On our second full day of training, we began to meet our chakra animals. My attention is immediately drawn to my belly chakra and Brown Bear. Although I am happy to see him, sadness washes over me. Instead of the wonderfully immense powerful arms he had when I first met him, today his arms are skinny and pale. I sense that Bear, reflecting my own feelings of uncertainty and insecurity in this foreign land, feels alone and abandoned. Bear wants me to know that I can reach out and embrace the other women in the group.

Noticing his solid feet, I see that when Bear stomps, the ground shakes and it sounds like thunder! Bear tells me, "You feel weak because you have cut off the circulation of life blood in your arms and legs." I look at my arms and legs. Skinny and pale, they feel weak. Bear says, "You need to eat lots of beets to get your circulation back and feel strong again."

Skipping and whistling, Bear encourages me to join him. Playing with him, I feel happier. Near the top of a hill, with his arms wrapped around me, Bear and I roll down the grassy slope entwined. Reaching the bottom, we separate and laugh loudly. Bear licks my face with unconditional love.

As our breathing becomes synchronized, with each breath we take, Bear and I increase in size and strength. We expand, filling the cosmos. Our breath becomes the wind of the Universe. Sensing that I am part of the rhythm of the Universe, my body feels innately connected to everyone and to everything. Bear tells me, "Remember this feeling!"

Smiling, he gives me another big bear hug before he leaves. Thanking him, I am aware that, even here, in Ireland, I am part of something and know that I am loved. Hearing the other women share their feelings and journeys in the group seems to rock me gently, allowing my defenses to lower so that I can connect with them and with lost pieces of myself.

Who Abandoned Whom?

The following morning, I woke with a feeling of having been abandoned and wondered where it came from. Yesterday, I felt so loved! Who abandoned me? Could it be that I have abandoned myself?

Later in the morning, as I was recounting in the group my journey with Bear and how the physical closeness with him made me feel loved, I described my joy in holding and rocking my children when they were small. I also remembered and related my long standing childhood desire to have a monkey as a pet. Each Christmas, picturing a monkey with its arms wrapped around me, a constant companion, I would send Santa my request. Did I really want a monkey or did I want the physical closeness I imagined a monkey would bring? As I voiced my truth in circle, I realized how important physical contact and connection have always been to me.

After the morning session, I felt more at ease in the group and realized that the process of facilitating the other women's journeys, witnessing their feelings and sharing mine were bringing me closer to them. It felt lovely to be in the cozy cottage with all of us squished together, our bodies touching and overlapping with a growing, easy familiarity.

The afternoon topic was polarity journeys, the meeting of opposing aspects. We finished up just before dinner. Excited about the session, at dinner we decided to continue our work into the evening.

I began the night as facilitator for a woman whose journey turned out to be unusually long, ending at 9:00 pm. Even though I had been eagerly anticipating what I would learn and see when it was my turn, I felt that I shouldn't ask for a ride back to the bed and breakfast so late in the evening. I'd wait until the following day to journey.

Back at the bed and breakfast, very disappointed, I tried to deal with my feelings rationally. But, I thought about the following morning. Sharing in the circle felt so important and I would not have a journey to share. While getting ready for bed, I heard myself say aloud, "I will never come here again without a car! I need freedom, independence and my own car!"

Lying in bed, I wondered why I couldn't ask someone
to wait for me. Did I feel that my needs weren't important
enough to inconvenience others? Raised in a family that
valued independence, I had always been reluctant to ask for
favors. Courtesy often took priority over self-expression.
Despite my strong desire to journey, it felt inappropriate
to ask someone to wait and drive me back to the bed and
breakfast at such a late hour.

Reflecting back over my feelings of abandonment in
the morning, I wondered if, at times, I had abandoned
the deepest desires of my inner self out of some misguided
notions about independence and strength. There may yet be
more gates I have to pass through - those related to fear of
dependency. Perhaps I'll learn to speak my needs clearly and
directly, instead of always considering the needs of others
first.

Bee Juice

*C*urious and eager to learn more about polarities in Deep Imagery, early next morning while still in bed, I toyed with the idea of meeting with my opposing aspects of "enough" and "not enough." Instantly, a small, folded piece of paper appeared as a symbol of not enough. Surprised, I ask why it was not an animal. Instead of answering, it unfolded into a bright yellow chrysanthemum bud, my least favorite flower. Noticing that the stem had been cut, and not wanting it to die, I placed it in a vase of water.

I watched as the flower absorbed the water and the petals opened.

I had difficulty staying focused on the imagery and impatiently I thought, "I can't do this!" and noticed a feeling of heaviness in my heart. I wished that Skunk, my delightful little heart animal, was with me. Swiftly, Skunk appeared, saying, "I'm here!" Pleased to see Skunk, my heart felt lighter.

My busy mind kept wandering from the image of the flower, and I become frustrated and irritated, wondering, "Why can't I do this by myself?" Trying to pay more attention to the flower, I desperately called for an animal guide of attention to assist me.

On the screen of my imagination, a big, round Loving Stone appeared and warmly told me, "It will be all right. You can do it. Just relax and don't work so hard at it." With Loving Stone near my heart, I became calm and again focused on the flower. Pulling off one petal at a time, I started to play the school-girl's game, He Loves Me, He Loves Me Not.

As I said, "He loves me," and was about to take the last yellow petal from the flower, a large, black, nasty-looking insect appeared from the center of the flower, frightening me.

Suddenly I thought, "This is all in my head! I am making this up!"

Maybe I should be doing this imagery session with someone else and not in bed by myself. Then I heard myself say, "No! This is a valid message, listen to it." Remembering that Loving Stone is present and that Skunk is watching patiently, I relaxed, feeling more sure of myself.

Returning my attention to the horrible black insect, I could see that it had big, sharp, pointed teeth. Flying toward me, it morphed into an enormous, menacing, black bee with furry legs and a large threatening stinger. Knowing that it is important to tell an animal guide how I feel, I anxiously said, "You are scary! I don't want you near me!" The bee was silent.

"I'm afraid you're going to sting me," I added a little more softly. Still the bee was silent, and we continued to look at each other. My body tightened with tension as I wondered what was going to happen next. No animal ever threatened to hurt me before.

Finally the giant Bee said, "I AM going to sting you! I'm going to sting you with Bee Juice." As Bee stung me, I felt my body being filled with golden Bee Juice and understood instantly. "You need to 'be' present with your feelings and all that happens within you." Smiling, Bee said, "I am stinging you with bee juice so that you can just be!"

Reflection of the Feminine

On the last day of training, I woke very early. Keeping my eyes shut, I remained still and thought over the past week. Feeling impatient and strangely stuck in some way, it was as if I were swimming under water, straining for the surface and air. I had the sensation that I was in my chest. I called upon Turtle, a good swimmer, who has helped me before. Swimming together, I felt more confident. We swam peacefully, but never reached the surface.

I rose and dressed, feeling grateful to have been part of

this wonderful group in this beautiful country. The women and Ireland had wound their way into my heart.With all of the sharing that had taken place, I realized how many feelings, memories and experiences each of us carries in our body. It had been a long and emotionally full week. I felt ready for the training to end and knew a sudden longing to be home.

As the group convened for the last circle of sharing, Steve led a group imagery session, where each of us met our animal of departure and re-entry. This animal would travel with us as we departed the training and help us transition back into our daily lives.

My animal guide was a beautiful brown and white sheep dog. I felt the warmth of his body as he stood close to me. Like so many sheep dogs I had watched in the fields of Ireland, he was alert and agile, strong and gentle. Sheep Dog lovingly told me, "I will let you be, but I will protect you so you don't wander off too far." I knew he would be the ideal travel companion as I left Ireland.

After the final circle, we all hugged and said good-bye. While placing my arms around the first woman and looking into her eyes, I was startled to see my own reflection. Her eyes were clearly mirrors for me. Instantly, I knew that each woman mirrored a piece of me. In a fleeting image, I saw that we were a circle of souls that were linked together. Our pains, our joys, our stories, our lives, each impacted the journey and the wholeness of the others. I left the training feeling enriched and empowered by the understanding of this special bond.

As my plane taxied down the Shannon runway with Sheep Dog beside me, I thought of my sisters in the group with affection. At the exact moment of lift off, as the plane's wheels lost contact with the Irish soil, I felt a physical ache in my chest and anxiety filled my body. Something very important was missing! I felt as if I'd left my pocketbook or passport or something else of great value behind. I quickly checked, but had both my pocketbook and my passport.

"What is it?" I asked Sheep Dog. "What have I left behind?" Sheep Dog smiled, and I realized that I felt the separation from the feminine energy that held me, rocked me and supported me during training. My heart felt the physical separation from the other women and from my connection with the intense, intuitive, feminine energy of the Irish Earth. Both mirrored for me the full power of the transformative feminine, re-awakening my own inner knowing of how I must live. I had just left something that my body recognized as essential for my life.

Back at home in Rockport, I realized that my trip to Ireland had been about more than just learning the techniques for Deep Imagery. I could sense that my body had absorbed many lessons, some of which were not yet known to me. I understood that the informal times of fun and laughter at meals, on walks and in the evenings had been as significant to our healing and growth as were the sharing of our journeys and feelings in the formal circle. A deep closeness had developed between us.

I had experienced a "drenching" of my being in Ireland - a deep soaking in the waters and world of the feminine.

The feminine not only because, other than Steve, everyone in the group was female, but also because the Irish Earth with its ancient mystic energy, intrinsic intuitive presence and lush green beauty felt deeply steeped in the feminine.

Living so close to the Earth, in sync with her tides and moon, had put me in touch with myself, nature and with others on a heart level. There, for one magical week, I lived life with rich simplicity in the reflection of the feminine.

About four weeks after the training, a photo postcard of Kinvara, Ireland, arrived from the training coordinator and I was delighted to see it. Her thoughtfulness was greatly appreciated. Placing the card immediately on my refrigerator door, I felt as if I had placed my open heart there. An image of the group instantly flashed in my mind, and my whole body reacted.

I could hear the sounds of their voices laughing and talking casually about everyday things. I could see each woman's face as she spoke and listened. A warm glance, falling tears and a gentle touch come to mind. They are all still with me! Every time my eyes gravitate to the postcard, it touches my whole body, reassuring me that the imagery training, the imagery training group and the town of Kinvara all really existed. And someplace, all of me really exists, too!

A few months later, as my plane landed at Shannon Airport for the second week of Deep Imagery Training, I felt a dramatic shift in my energy. Stepping back into the feminine energy of Ireland, my breath suddenly felt fuller and my heart thudded solidly. A woman from the group, kindly met me at the airport. It was wonderful to see her, and she drove me to a small bed and breakfast in the center of Kinvara where I had a reservation.

From the window in my room, I can see vast stretches of green grass and emerald hills rolling endlessly out toward the ocean. Stone walls form a checkerboard pattern and a gentle mist becomes a gorgeous rainbow that spans the sky.

My heart feels more fully alive than usual, and I realize how busy I am, externally and internally, when I am at home. Here I can slow down and "just be," with myself and others.

Already, I had been given many gifts in preparation for the up-coming week of training. The feminine energy of the land, friendship, poetry, the soft rain, the sea, the sun and a gorgeous rainbow all welcomed me! I felt ready in a way I had not when coming into the first week of training.

Arriving at the cottage, where I was delighted to be staying this time, I had the distinct feeling of coming home. The rich green Earth seemed to rise right up through my shoes and feet, bathing every cell of my body with its moisture. My legs and feet felt stronger than usual, almost as if they had taken root.

Walking the rough stone path to the cottage, it seemed like the past few months had disappeared, as if I'd been sleeping and now woke to another morning during the initial week of training. My body slid right back into the recognition of the sights, smells and sounds.

With eagerness, I looked forward to continuing the training and reuniting with my "sisters." It was such an extraordinary group of women with whom I could explore all the different aspects of myself through the fascinating process of Deep Imagery. To be loved and to share the deep shadows of our lives with no judgment is a rare gift of the feminine. In the light of the love I had already experienced with the group, parts of me were beginning to come to life, parts I had long forgotten.

In my first Deep Imagery journey during the second week of training, I asked for an animal guide for whatever journey needed to happen for my growth and healing to take place. Grey Wolf came as a strong, but nurturing guide.

Howling with Grey Wolf

I watched the beautiful creature as she moved in a circle, matting down the grass as she walked. With great attention, she taught me how to make a warm nest in the grass. Grey Wolf told me, "You have the ability to make your nest - a safe, warm spot - anywhere."

Watching Grey Wolf, I sensed that I did have this skill. Practicing with her, I made a comfy place for myself. Grey Wolf's observing eyes surveyed my nest with approval. Snuggled in my nest, we watched the day quietly end and twilight approach.

"You have forgotten your voice," Grey Wolf told me. She pointed her snout to the sky and howled. I shuddered as her howl quavered through the night sky. At her insistence, I joined her and we raised our voices together.

When I heard the wild sound of my own howl, robust and clear, I realized what a genuine part of me and my connection with other wolves it is. My spirit danced as I continued to howl.

At her invitation, I entered Grey Wolf's strong body. I could see my large, beautiful paws against the white, snow-covered Earth. I walked with a spring in my step. We ran and played together, and I relished the freedom. Solid and centered, Grey Wolf's energy felt very good to me.

As Grey Wolf, I know what to do and how to live. Her relationship to other wolves is instinctual and simple. Grey Wolf's howl lets her stance be known. She has great strength and endurance alone, and yet Grey Wolf is part of a pack. Together, the wolves work cooperatively for food and survival. Grey Wolf reminds me, "You have all this instinct, voice and ability inside your own body. Remember who you are."

That night several of us went to the pub and I heard myself laughing without restraint, having great fun. Invigorated by my journey with Grey Wolf, I felt like the "me" I had forgotten, the younger, freer me.

The women teased me about my white running shoes, which I also wore during the first training week. We all knew that while in Ireland, my "white wellies," as they humorously called them, didn't run. Instead, they climbed over stone walls, trudged through deep seaweed tossed up on the cottage lawn at high tide, traversed muddy paths and tramped through green cow and sheep pastures. Looking down at my white wellies under the table, we all laughed. They had matured to a rich, deep green!

Deciding that I would make a translation dictionary with the assistance of my Irish sisters, our fun continued. Our dictionary would include all the Irish words and expressions I didn't understand. Our laughter rang throughout the pub.

As we sang Irish songs, I mentioned that I had not heard one Irish song that wasn't sad. The women decided to find an Irish song to sing for me that was happy. Quite pleased with herself, one woman thought of one. We all laughed when we heard the last line, in which the young lover, missing her dead beau, jumps into the grave with him! I felt accepted, loved, "part of the pack." My heart was happy.

Through the Eyes of Snake

*W*e took the next afternoon off to explore St. Colman's Well and Cave on the Burren, the barren, rocky area in the western part of Ireland. Crossing over the stone covered ground and hills of the Burren, we slowly hiked up toward one of the highest points of land where the cave was located. In contrast to the barren stone below, the Earth there was thickly covered with clover and green moss and sprinkled with small alpine flowers.

A thick slab of ancient stone was poised horizontally as

an altar. Next to it, covered in deep moss, was a time-worn baptismal bowl hollowed out of stone. The word 'primeval' came to mind, and I knew my feet were treading on sacred ground. A short climb higher, in a protected spot, was the cave. Chiseled out of the rock by nature, it was almost hidden from the eye in passing.

As I crouched to enter this small, ancient cave by myself, I was uncertain as to what I would find. Slightly dark, the inside of the cave was about six feet across and not quite tall enough for me to stand. Squatting in the middle of the cave with my eyes closed, I sensed the energy of those who were here before me. The energy whirled through me, making me tingle slightly. Closing my eyes, I could see streaks of black, then white and then color, flashes of the lives of old inhabitants of this cave. There were ancient humans, snakes and other animals. The intense energy traveled through me, leaving me dizzy and dazed.

Opening my eyes, I attempted to center myself. In the dim light, my eyes became fixed on a shape on the cave wall. A snake's head about the size of a human head extended out in front of me from the stone-wall. Looking again, I could see that it was actually a rock, yet I sensed the presence of Snake, my forehead animal of intuition and knowing. An electric current ran through my body, connecting me to the past, the present and the future, all at the same time. It was communion with the entire Universe!

Making my way back to the entrance of the cave, the bright light of day hurt my eyes. Squinting, I stepped out of the cave and gazed at the lush green countryside in the distance. Scanning the horizon, I recognized the view. Awe-struck, my rational mind was stunned into stillness, and the measurement of time as I have known it did not exist.

I was gazing at the same deep green landscape that I had seen through the eyes of Snake in one of my initial journeys, long before I came to Ireland. My body vibrated with recognition and time blurred and ran together. Following the trail down off the Burren, back to the road where we left our van, my spirits soared. I was in the right place, and I knew I was on the right Path!

Owning My Voice, Heart and Power with a Golden, Celtic Twist!

*F*or the next two days, we continued to meet our chakra animals and practiced facilitating as others met theirs. I encountered four guides, all different than they'd appeared before.

When I addressed my throat chakra, calling out to Little Bird's Beak, I was surprised when two huge lips suddenly appeared, saying loudly, "Hello!" The lips told me that Little Bird's Beak was no longer loud enough and that they were my new guides.

At first I wasn't sure whether I liked having these new, very vocal guides. I missed my gentle, melodious Little Bird's Beak.

"Pay attention to your throat and feel all the feelings there," The Huge Lips strongly advised me. Demonstrating how vociferous they can be, they laughed loudly and began to make a deafening, lip-smacking sound. It was a sound that, if made by a child in a social setting, would evoke disapproval. I was instantly annoyed with this new guide.

Hearing the noise, however, reminded me that as a child I was taught to be verbally reserved, careful not to say anything that might offend anyone. I couldn't always say what I honestly thought, and so it seemed my feelings, thoughts and ideas must be somehow wrong.

The Huge Lips smiled and laughingly told me that there was nothing wrong with what I felt or thought, and that my observations were often quite right. Their fun-loving spirit, kindness and ease with themselves quickly built a fondness within me for my new friends.

Becoming one with The Huge Lips and experiencing their energy, my throat felt wider and when I spoke, I could hear that my own voice had a stronger tone and more volume. Joyfully, The Huge Lips told me, "We are here with you when you need us." About to say good-bye, an insight came to me - I have passed along to my daughter a similar caution about her own self-expression. I understood that when I stop inhibiting myself, I will free her from this same expectation. I thanked The Huge Lips for this important message, both for myself and for Ariana.

At dinner that evening, the whole group, enthralled by the changes in our animals, decided to continue sessions into the evening.

When I called forth an animal guide, the area around my heart chakra felt constricted. Instead of Skunk, I saw a different little animal emerging. It was an anteater! Anteater said, "Notice my head. It is very small." Touching his heart he said, "Today your heart is more important than your head. When you are in your head, you can't feel your heart." Smiling, he leaned toward me and whispered, "The connection between your heart and your throat is vital! Always say what you feel in your heart."

As he spoke, I watched a ribbon join my throat and my heart. Once connected, my heart began to increase in size, extending all the way across my chest. With my arms spread out to the sides, my heart reached all the way from one fingertip to the other.

"Just feel what a large heart you have," he continued with a smile. I was grateful to Anteater for his final reminder, "You must always remember to leave your big heart open."

In my session the next day, I experienced a tightness in my solar plexus, the area governing my will, my power and my knowing when and how to act. Buffalo appeared, this time as a female accompanied by her small calf. Buffalo told me that my rib cage was too crowded for both of them, and I observed while she widened it so that her calf was able to stand beside her. I was intrigued by this image of Mother Buffalo with her calf, but also somehow saddened.

"Let that sadness come," said Mother Buffalo.

"I am sad for the little one, but I don't know why," I told her. Initially, I assumed I was sad for her calf because it seemed so vulnerable on its wobbly legs. But on second thought, I realized that my sadness related to leaving my own little one, my daughter, at home.

Knowing that imagery is to be experienced, not analyzed, I just let myself sit with these feelings. Stretching my solar plexus further, Mother Buffalo made more room for calf and herself. "You need to own all your power," she said.

Stroking Mother Buffalo's thick brown fur, I watched as her warmth and sturdiness formed a stream of love and power that flowed directly into my body, moving through my solar plexus, heart and throat. Mother Buffalo encouraged me to recognize the connection between these three chakras. In doing so, I experienced a new charge of energy and authority within my body as a whole.

Next, addressing my crown, the area of spirituality, I saw a beautiful golden pyramid showering brilliant amber light over my head and down through my body. Golden Pyramid, my new crown guide, had come to illuminate my way. Wrapped in her warm rays like a soft blanket, I felt comfortable, safe and protected.

Golden Pyramid promised to be with me whenever I chose to be aware of her. Saturating me with golden brilliance, she left my body with a residual inner glow and peacefulness.

Late that evening, while looking back over my journeys with my throat, heart, solar plexus and crown chakra guides, I marveled at the changes I had experienced. My four guides reclaimed for me a stronger voice, offered me a more intrinsic connection with my heart, reconfirmed my sense of personal will, and recharged my spirit with an intensity unknown to me before.

With their great kindness and wisdom, Huge Lips, Anteater, Mother Buffalo and Golden Pyramid strengthened and softened me, deftly preparing me for the culmination of my trip to Ireland.

Leper Woman

*T*he agenda for the day was a council of our chakra
animal guides. My first council was such a powerful, life-
altering journey that I greatly looked forward to what this
one would hold for me.

My group of four was excited to be journeying
together; the combination of women seemed just right. Our
energy was charged with laughter, eagerness and anticipa-
tion as we settled ourselves in our room to begin. As if pre-
determined by the Universe, the order in which we would

journey became very clear. Each journey would layer upon the preceding one, jostling the feelings and setting the stage for the next.

The first woman's journey concerned her birth. The second woman's centered on birth and death. Mine was about re-birth. The fourth woman's journey focused on relationships and new life.

When it was my turn, I eagerly asked my crown chakra guide if it would be appropriate to have a council. My new crown guide, Golden Pyramid, agreed. Although Golden Pyramid had only been with me for one day, I felt safe in her presence and comfortable with her decision. Curiously, I also noticed two bumps, like the ones found on the top of a giraffe's head, appearing with Golden Pyramid. It was clear that both The Bumps and Golden Pyramid would guide my journey.

Golden Pyramid began by explaining that she needed to send her light to my heart. Upon hearing her words, I suddenly experienced a deep pain in my chest. Golden Pyramid's shower of warm light illuminated a golden string attached to the top of my heart. Focusing on the string, I noticed that it was very taut and tugged at my heart. Watching it pull, my heart felt such pain I thought it might break! Golden Pyramid reassured me that my heart would not break, but that it needed my attention.

Suddenly I realized that I must be afraid to look at some heartache. "Yes, we have been holding this ache for you," Golden Pyramid said. A profound sadness washed through my body. Although I didn't understand what

Golden Pyramid was referring to, I felt there wasn't room in my heart to hold the size of this hurt. Together, Golden Pyramid and The Bumps assured me that there was enough room. With Golden Pyramid shining her warm light directly on my heart, I could see that my heart was like a cavernous well, with a flight of stairs descending into its darkness. A profound fear washed over me, and I lost all awareness of my surroundings.

"Am I to go down into the darkness?" I asked Golden Pyramid. Saying nothing, Golden Pyramid continued to bathe me in her radiance. I repeated my question.

"Yes."

My fear rises and my heart pounds. Desperately, I ask Golden Pyramid and The Bumps if they will come with me. They agree, and with much trepidation, I timidly place one foot onto the top step. The stairs seem creaky. Everything is totally dark, and I'm afraid I'll fall. I cling tightly to the railing and go quietly, carefully, step by step. My legs start to shake and weakness spreads out from behind my knees. Terror fills my body and it's hard to breathe.

Very slowly, I move down onto the next, dark step. Nameless horror lurks all around me and I'm terrified that something is waiting down there to grab me. I try to pay attention to every side, but I don't know from which direction the danger will come and it's difficult to make my legs move. My feet and legs have turned to stone, my heart pounds ever harder and my breath is shallow. I feel so alone!

Remembering that Golden Pyramid is with me, I ask her for reassurance. The instant I focus my attention on her instead of the darkness, her brilliant light showers over me and I don't feel so alone anymore. I begin to feel safer, almost as if I have a glass dome of protective warmth around me. Taking a slow, deep breath, I continue my descent. Moving just ahead of Golden Pyramid, I am in almost total darkness.

I suddenly recall a dream I had many years ago, and it plays out on the darkness before me as if on a screen. I see myself on a dark stairway, clinging terrified to a handrail, as a human-sized bat brushes its furry, bony, black body against my cheek. As the image fades, I ask Golden Pyramid if there is something I need to know about this dream.

"You need to face your fear so you won't be afraid of the dark," she responds.

On the screen of darkness before me appears another scene, not a dream, but remembered reality. I see myself, a little girl lying in bed. Five or six, I'm terrified that something in the dark will grab me. I hold perfectly still and breathe very shallowly, hoping not to be noticed. Standing on the stair, the body of the adult me relives the experience. My heart races, I can barely breathe, and I'm frozen with fear!

Feeling alone and vulnerable, I ask, "Golden Pyramid where are you? I don't see you." There is no response, and sheer terror grips my body!

Finally, I remember my other guides for this journey. I call out for The Bumps and discover that they are now on top of my head. For reassurance, I want to reach up and touch The Bumps, but I am petrified and my body feels incapable of movement. Very slowly, I inch my arms up to my head and with trembling hands, search desperately for The Bumps.

Finding them, I realize that they are actually buttons that open and close my eye lids! When I press these unique buttons, my eyes open and light shines out like retractable headlights on a car. This strikes me as wildly funny in the midst of dark fear, and I start to laugh. I have my very own headlights!

Golden Pyramid tells me that when I'm afraid of the dark, I can flash my lights. Reassured, I practice pressing the buttons several times and watch as my eyes pop open and my lights flash! I am struck with gales of laughter when I see myself turn into one of those soft plastic stress dolls. Squeeze my tummy and my tongue and eyes will pop out! The more I laugh, the more I relax and my laughter chases away my fear.

Without warning, the doll turns into the human-sized bat from my old dream. In the semi-darkness, I see Bat's big black eyes and pointed ears. He is skinny and bony and has sharp teeth. Bat wants me to climb onto his back. Terrified, I don't want to touch Bat or have Bat touch me. The next instant I find myself hanging upside down, bat-style, from the ceiling of a cave! The cave is dark and damp and I hear the sound of thousands of other bats. My heart pounds as the fear returns.

"This is my home," Bat tells me. "Don't be afraid."

Looking down at myself, I don't see any skin. I am just bones and tissue and black! I don't want to be hanging here and I don't want to be a bat. I say so, fast and loud, and the scene changes.

Now I find myself flying as a bat outside the cave across the night sky. I am pleased with the openness and freedom. The black sky easily becomes my friend and I circle through it with delight. My mind can't grasp the change in my feelings, but my body understands it perfectly. I relax even more, and see that Bat is flying near me. He shows me how he flies, darting and changing direction with lightning speed. Taken with the beauty of his motion, I start to appreciate Bat's unique abilities.

"No one sees the moon the way I see it!" Bat says proudly. Darting right in front of the sparkling white moon, he almost seems to touch it. His enjoyment of the clear night air and his relationship to the black sky and the dazzling moonlight are irresistible. Bat's joy in being himself enchants me and my fear of Bat is replaced with genuine fondness as I watch him glide blissfully through the striking sky.

I ask my new friend Bat if there is anything else he needs to show me. Directing my attention to my heart again, he encourages me to continue down the stairs. He wants me to befriend the darkness. Feeling more comfortable with the dark after our magical flight together, I agree.

Nearing the bottom of the stairs, I peer through the dim light. In the shadows are several scary-looking, human-like forms. I force myself to take the final step down into this murky dungeon. Standing on the floor in the blackness, I hold very still, just as I did in bed when I was a small child. I want to hide! This darkness does not feel the same as the dark sky in which I was just flying so freely with Bat. I stand perfectly still, hoping to be invisible.

In a glimmer of light, I see a skeleton on the dirt floor. Empty eye sockets seem to follow me as I hesitantly take one step forward. Quickly glancing around, I see other skeletons leaning against the walls. I am in a catacomb. Over on the right in the shadows, crouched in a dusty indentation in the wall, I see a woman wrapped in an old, dirty blanket or hooded robe. She is a Leper.

Bat appears beside me and directs me to speak to her. Timidly, I do so. Afraid that Bat will ask me to touch her, I tell him that I don't want to go near this Leper Woman. Although frightened, I am fascinated by her. I continue trying to see her in the dim light. I recognize this woman from somewhere. She is familiar, but I can't quite place her.

As she turns toward me, a sliver of light grazes her face and I see her wounds, scars and oozing sores. A few straggles of dirty matted hair escape from her hood. She is unkempt, uncared-for, forgotten down here. Her soft, deep, brown eyes are sad.

Slowly, compassion stirs within me for this woman left in the dark to rot. But I remain fearful. As the woman unfolds her arms and opens her robe, I see a baby clutched close to her heart. Sick with despair, I see that the baby is skinny, scarred and also disfigured with leprosy. She turns the baby toward me.

"No!" I start to cry. In this instant, I know that the baby she holds is actually my baby – the baby I miscarried nine years ago! Grief and terror simultaneously seize my body. I can't bear to look, yet my eyes cannot leave this baby.

"Will you wash the baby?" Bat asks me. Turning my head, I can't face this task. I want to run away! It is only my relationship with Bat that keeps me here. With great conflict and hesitation, I do what Bat has asked. Slowly, my hands reach out for the baby. Nearby, I see a basin of sparkling, warm water and a soft cloth, and soon I am washing the baby gently. The warm water not only cleanses the baby's skin of dirt, but miraculously clears the wounds and scars. Amazed, I watch as its body fills out and the flesh becomes pink and plump.

"Will you bury the baby?" the woman asks in a soft, pleading voice. Her request takes me back to the time I had my first miscarriage. I feel my sadness and my despair. I see myself reach into the toilet, holding the blood clots, aching to know which one is my baby. The image broadens to include the other two miscarriages, and my whole body relives my unspeakable grief.

Once more the picture expands and I see myself newly married to Guntis. I am pregnant. I remember my first abortion. And my second. Wrenching sorrow wells up from within me. Expanding still further, the image now includes me in my early twenties, during that first abortion. I am overcome with anguish as my body moves through each conception and each loss.

"You need to bury your babies," Bat tenderly instructs me. Distraught, I tell Bat that I can not carry so many coffins.

"I will help you," Bat says soothingly.

I now see six babies in the catacomb. I know they are mine. With great love I bathe each baby with Leper Woman standing by my side. As I finish bathing my last baby, glancing at Leper Woman, I see with astonishment that simultaneously her sores and wounds also heal and disappear.

With a knowing smile, she reaches out to stroke my cheek and offers to help me. Together, we ceremoniously wrap each one of my babies in a beautiful velvet cloth.

"I am sorry I could not help them live," I say, as warm, healing tears flow down my cheeks.

"You did nothing wrong," she lovingly responds.

Golden Pyramid suddenly appears, shining her light through my body, and flooding my womb with her miraculous healing energy.

"I didn't know that I was still carrying them. I didn't realize how heavy my heart has been, and I didn't know what to do with my babies." I whisper softly to Golden Pyramid, Bat and the Woman.

"We know. This is why we have come to help you." The Woman, like a Fairy God Mother to me now, holds my hand. "Now it is time to let them go," she says.

I gaze with a new mother's adoration at my six babies, now honored, loved and peaceful. As tears roll down my cheeks, I hear myself saying to my little ones, "I love you, I love you all." My heart is relieved when The Woman reassures me that Mother Earth will take good care of my babies.

"We will all fly with Bat to bury your babies," she tells me. The Woman assists me in placing my six babies carefully on Bat's strong back and with the last one secure, the two of us slide onto Bat's wings. Flying with Bat, I watch the green of Ireland slowly pass below. My attention is drawn to a quiet spot beneath a tree, where the Earth is covered with thick, beautiful Irish moss.

In ancient times, women would come here to the moss monthly to bleed, their feminine blood flowing back, back to Mother Earth. This is a sacred place. I know this is where I am to bury my babies.

Bat lands smoothly and waits patiently while The Woman and I lovingly remove my babies one by one from his back. In a procession of honor, we carry each baby to the moss-covered ground surrounding the tree. With The Woman standing at my side, Bat, messenger of hope and guardian of re-birth, dips his wings in tribute to new life.

All my chakra animals gather in a circle around me. I feel their tremendous life and their unending support. Kneeling, quietly humming a lullaby, I cradle each baby in my arms, swathing it with the soft moss. Supported by the masculine action of Bat and held by the feminine, kissing my little ones tenderly, I settle them to rest in the arms of Mother Earth.

Relinquishing my last baby to Mother Earth's rich, Irish soil, I am surprised as beautiful, fragrant flowers spring forth! It is as if Mother Earth had been waiting for my babies, needing them for her flowers to grow. Mother Earth welcomes my babies, saying affectionately, "Indeed, I have been waiting for them."

My maternal heart mends at last and my body is flooded with peace, knowing that all that is, flowers, Irish moss, Bat and people are all One. That which has form and that which is formless all share the same energy. I hear Mother Earth's loving words to me: "When you walk upon the Earth and see my flowers, remember, you will see,

your babies . . .
my babies . . .
all our babies!"

Heart's Treasures

*T*he day after my encounter with Leper Woman, the training group surprised me with a touching celebration of my fiftieth birthday, presenting me with a pair of my very own, authentic Irish wellies! My heart overflowed with feelings of being accepted and loved, with the importance of my healing journey recognized and honored. It was a glorious way to celebrate a pivotal point in my life.

Today, years later, near the door to my garden, my beautiful Irish Wellies wait for me. And in the early morning light of soft days, I slip them on and walk in the garden, where I see my Grandfather among his flowers. Our hearts unite in our mutual understanding of the real treasure these women have given me, that of witnessing and acknowledging the journey of my soul coming home.

I see my Grandfather smile as we both look down at my wellies. On the sides of them, the women in my group, in joyful reverence, had painted beautiful flowers so that when I walk on the Earth, when I see flowers, I will see . . .

her babies . . .

my babies. . .

all of our babies!

Afterward

I believe that the Universe, with its infinite wisdom, not only sent my Grandfather from the Land of the Dead to bring me back to life, but to lead me to Deep Imagery and to Ireland.

It was through the miraculously precise and sensitive process of Deep Imagery, with my animal guides skillfully nurturing me, that I was able to rebalance the feminine and masculine within myself and heal my losses. Allowing me to access my inner knowing, authentically, on a body level,

Deep Imagery aided me exquisitely in transforming my core understanding of the essential feminine and its natural energies.

Everything that happened from the moment I saw the brochure in the book store supported and moved me forward to that place and moment in time, when, held by the Irish feminine, I could befriend Leper Woman in the dark. Only by recognizing and honoring that part of myself could I embrace my six babies and release them to the loving care of Mother Earth, finally bringing peace to my heart and soul.

Deep Imagery guided me to experience the oneness of all living things and Mother Earth as the "ultimate mother." Rekindling the sacred dimensions of the feminine, Deep Imagery and my animals deftly and lovingly, helped me to weave the mysteries of the feminine *permanently* into my consciousness and into the fabric of my being. I now remember more fully who I am.

Our stories of the deep feminine and the sharing of our stories hold healing for both the teller and the witness. We must teach our daughters and our sons, as well as continue our own learnings about the value of the feminine. I encourage each woman to accept the invitation that is offered to her to expand her knowledge of herself and her connection to all living things.

These invitations for descent and reconnection often come up unannounced, whether through struggles with conception, like mine, or through a life-threatening illness, depression, traumatic loss or other major life change. Not every woman's search will lead her to the same place. Each of us must discover and follow with reverence our own unique way.

In sharing our soul journeys and encounters with the feminine, we honor the tremendous gift of balance the feminine brings, not only to our personal lives, but in a larger sense, to our society as a whole. By voicing our stories, we help to bring the deep feminine and its sacred gifts into its rightful place in our culture, inspiring broader hope and change.

I thank you for witnessing my story.
Phyllis Brooks Licis

Acknowledgements

I am thankful to Great Spirit for guiding me on my path of healing, bringing peace to my heart and womb and helping me to restore my life to genuine vitality.

I will forever be grateful to my husband, Guntis, for his ability to hear and honor my soul's awakening and for his courage in making the required leap of faith. I admire his willingness for me to share his part of my story and his enthusiasm about my writing this book.

Without the gift of our son, Eriks, with whom I first experienced the joys of motherhood, I would not have known how to mother. Without the grace and tenacity of our daughter, Ariana, I would not have had the opportunity to experience the gift of pregnancy and then the miracle of birth - hers and my own.

My love and appreciation goes to my Grandfather for his passionate liveliness and the deep, organic, Earth-connection which he awakened in me.

Many thanks to Dr. James Eckles for his daring and determined spirit, which steadied me, as I made my way through my inner depths, recognizing myself as a female, a woman and a mother.

I feel blessed to have had family and friends who have taught me throughout my life.

A special thank you goes to my sister, Beverly Wiley. A nurturing "second mother" to my children and myself, her creative, loving presence in our lives has always been like a sheltering tree. A heartfelt thanks, also, goes to my brother, Donald Brooks, for helping me embark on this life-sustaining adventure of imagery training in Ireland. The magical sunflower journal he gave me for my first week of training, held the very seeds for this book.

The insightful comments, suggestions and kind words from my friends, Connie Wayman, Sallie Felton and Claire Crosby, in the reading of my first draft, encouraged me to tell my story in this book and reinforced my belief that women need to share more of their life stories.

I am grateful to my friend, Lynn Tipton, for patiently

and graciously walking with me through my journals, assisting me in designing my words with love and dignity, honoring with the view of a Reiki Master the sacredness of my story.

To Gail Harris, an author, wife and mother, I entrusted my heart and story during the initial editing of my book. Her clear eye for structure and order, balanced with her warm, respectful approach and awareness of the feminine spiritual journey were important as we transformed my story to book form.

Inez Castor's finely-honed editorial skills, her intuitive relationship with the written word, along with her visceral understanding of the sacred were vital during the final editing of my book in bringing forth my story's full voice. Our paths over-lapped in an unexpected, remarkable manner and I am grateful to Inez for hearing and embracing my animals and my journey.

Many thanks to Mary Diggin for her tremendous energy and design talent and her brilliant use of my paintings for this book, as she formatted my book to printed form.

I have enormous gratitude to Dr. Eligio Stephen Gallegos for bringing his work, Deep Imagery (The Personal Totem Pole Process©) to the world and for teaching it in a manner that allowed me to experience "the teacher as a student" and "the student as a teacher." Deep Imagery is a tremendous tool for opening the door to one's creativity and inner healing. It has lead me to a more authentic way of being and restored genuine meaning to my life. I am honored to have had the opportunity to study with Steve and to have been able to assist him in this compelling, transformational, imagery process. I extend a sincere thank you to him for believing in the power of my story, for encouraging me to write this book and for publishing it as I gave birth to my written voice as a woman.

Last but not least, I give my most sincere respect and appreciation to all of my animal guides for their gentle approach and exquisite timing, as they stood by, quietly and patiently, allowing me to meet my darkness and my light.

I am extremely grateful for having been able to hear the call of the deep feminine and journey into the mysteries of this once foreign land. Held by the feminine and supported by my animal guides, I was able, once again, to embrace my babies and myself as a mother and a woman. With my arms and heart wide open, I walk tall and know who I am.

About the Author

As an artist, wife and mother, Phyllis embraces all with her warmth and openness, and passionately encourages each of us to trust in an inner knowing, as we see and give voice to the lessons in our own life stories.

Obtaining a Masters Degree in Social Work and certification in Family Therapy, she also studied art at Boston's Museum of Fine Arts School, using her love of oils for, what she calls, "a medium of the soul".

"Smitten by Imagery", Phyllis trained in Ireland with Dr. Eligios Stephen Gallegos, Ph.D., founder and pioneer of Deep Imagery. As a certified Deep Imagery Workshop Leader and Trainer, Phyllis is recognized by the International Institute of Visualization Research for her work with Deep Imagery.

With over 25 years of clinical experience, with an expertise in individual therapy and couples' counseling, Phyllis has learned that being in "right-relationship" with ourselves and others means listening to the wisdom of our bodies and following the truth of our hearts.

Recently moving from her beloved home in Rockport, MA to the warm sands of Ft Myers, FL, she devotes her time (when not working to protect manatees!) to teaching Deep Imagery workshops and training other therapists, healing professionals, artists and lay people how to use their own spontaneous images in the process of Deep Imagery.

Her creativity and sense of humor enrich her work with men and women as Phyllis presents Introductory lectures, Deep Imagery Sessions, Workshops and Certified Deep Imagery Trainings through out the United States, demonstrating how to "listen within and invite our soul to speak"!

For more information, visit
www.PhyllisBrooksDeepImagery.com

Resources

For information on Deep Imagery:

International Institute for Visualization Research
PO Box 632
Velarde NM 87582
www.deepimagery.org
www.facebook.com/deepimagery
office@deepimagery.org

Eligio Stephen Gallegos, PhD,
PO Box 468
Velarde NM 87572
www.esgallegos.com
info@esgallegos.com

Books on Deep Imagery from Moon Bear Press:

Control and Obedience: The Human Illness
by E.S. Gallegos Ph.D. (2012)

Chakra Power Animals: The Living Energies of the Chakras
by E.S. Gallegos Ph.D. (2012)

The Personal Totempole Process: Animal Imagery, the Chakras and Psychotherapy
by E.S. Gallegos Ph.D. Kindle Edition (2012)

Animals of The Four Windows:
Integrating Thinking, Sensing, Feeling and Imagery
by E.S. Gallegos Ph.D. ISBN: 0944164404

Into Wholeness: The Path of Deep Imagery
by E.S. Gallegos Ph.D. ISBN 978-0944164228

Little Ed and Golden Bear
by E.S. Gallegos Ph.D. ISBN 978-0944164068

The Circus Cage: A Journey of Transformation
by Rosalie G. Douglas. ISBN 978-0944164020

www.ingramcontent.com/pod-product-compliance
Lightning Source LLC
Chambersburg PA
CBHW060347090426
42734CB00011B/2063